W9-BQM-108

Gramley Library
Salem College
Winston-Salem, NC 27108

ELIZABETH BISHOP

ELIZABETH BISHOP

The Restraints of Language

C. K. DORESKI

New York   Oxford
OXFORD UNIVERSITY PRESS
1993

Gramley Library
Salem College
Winston-Salem, NC 27108

Oxford University Press

Oxford   New York   Toronto
Delhi   Bombay   Calcutta   Madras   Karachi
Kuala Lumpur   Singapore   Hong Kong   Tokyo
Nairobi   Dar es Salaam   Cape Town
Melbourne   Auckland   Madrid

and associated companies in
Berlin   Ibadan

Copyright © 1993 by Oxford University Press, Inc.

Published by Oxford University Press, Inc.,
200 Madison Avenue, New York, New York 10016

Oxford is a registered trademark of Oxford University Press

All rights reserved. No part of this publication may be reproduced,
stored in a retrieval system, or transmitted, in any form or by any means,
electronic, mechanical, photocopying, recording, or otherwise,
without the prior permission of Oxford University Press.

Library of Congress Cataloging-in-Publication Data
Doreski, Carole Kiler.
Elizabeth Bishop : the restraints of language / C. K. Doreski.
p.   cm.   Includes bibliographical references and index.
ISBN 0-19-507966-3
1. Bishop, Elizabeth, 1911–1979—Criticism and interpretation.
I. Title.   PS3503.I785Z635   1993   811′.52—dc20   92-30152

Since this page cannot legibly accommodate all the permissions, the following page constitutes
an extension of the copyright page.

2 4 6 8 9 7 5 3 1

Printed in the United States of America
on acid-free paper

Grateful acknowledgment is made to the following:

Farrar, Straus, and Giroux for excerpts from *The Collected Prose* by Elizabeth Bishop, copyright © 1984 by Alice Helen Methfessel and excerpts from *The Complete Poems 1927–1979* by Elizabeth Bishop, copyright © 1979, 1983 by Alice Helen Methfessel.

Excerpts from the unpublished writing of Elizabeth Bishop used with the permission of her Estate, © 1993, by Alice Helen Methfessel.

Special Collections of the Vassar College Library for permission to quote from drafts of "The Moose," "The End of March," and "Cape Breton" by Elizabeth Bishop.

Houghton Library, Harvard University, for permission to quote from the Elizabeth Bishop–Robert Lowell correspondence.

Special Collections, Olin Library, Washington University, for permission to quote from the Elizabeth Bishop–Anne Stevenson correspondence as well as the Elizabeth Bishop–May Swenson correspondence.

R. P. Knudson on behalf of the Literary Estate of May Swenson for permission to quote from the May Swenson–Elizabeth Bishop correspondence, Special Collections, Olin Library, Washington University Library.

The Publishers and Trustees of Amherst College for selections from *The Poems of Emily Dickinson*, Thomas H. Johnson, ed., Cambridge, Mass.: The Belknap Press of Harvard University Press. Copyright © 1951, 1955, 1979, 1983 by the President and Fellows of Harvard College.

Alfred A. Knopf, Inc. for selections from *Collected Poems* by Wallace Stevens. Copyright 1954 by Wallace Stevens; from *The Necessary Angel* by Wallace Stevens. Copyright 1951 by Wallace Stevens. Reprinted by permission of Alfred A. Knopf, Inc.

Parts of Chapter 2 appeared as "Elizabeth Bishop: Author(ity) and the Rhetoric of (Un)Naming," *The Literary Review* 35 (Spring 1992).

For Bill

Preface

For a time I feared this study, like the stream in Bishop's "To the Botequim & Back," would keep "descending, talk[ing] as it goes," disappear into a cavern, and never be seen again [CPr, 79]. I once had reason to believe myself among the first critics to contemplate the entirety of Bishop's career. Long before the publication of *Geography III*, I had spent hours at the Boston Public Library searching through *Life and Letters To-day*, *Partisan Review*, and the *New Yorker*, tracking down Elizabeth Bishop through her then-uncollected work.

My preoccupation originated the evening I abandoned a Bailey's soda (a treat for a Californian new to the city of Boston) in favor of a reading by (as the Boston *Globe* put it) "the poet of 'The Fish.'" She arrived flustered, distracted, and forty-five minutes late. She anxiously read through four poems, glanced up, and prepared for a hasty retreat. Brought back to the microphone, Bishop acquiesced to one question: Would she read "Sestina"? A lifetime of working to bring her knowledge and her poetics into mutual focus had generated a surface tension powerful enough to convert the rough draft "Early Sorrows" into the tonally perfect "Sestina," averting through formal and rhetorical dexterity the temptations of sentiment. Bishop's reading confirmed my sense that the restraints of language shaped the tone, tensions, and even the topics of her poetry. Rather than an escape from emotion this represented its liberation not only from bathos but from the high ironies of

modernism, which had become as perfunctory as Victorian sentiment.

My title refers to both an aesthetic and a temperament in which
restraint is a positive virtue. I hope to persuade readers that restraint for this poet is a necessary element in the relationship she
finds between language and life. To ignore either the sincere buoy-
ancy or the equally sincere despair of her "awful but cheerful"
world is to regard Bishop as a victim, not a poet. The balanced
terms of this paradox offer one example of her effort to balance
the delicate tonalities of her life and her art. I repeatedly found
myself examining critical studies that portrayed an Elizabeth
Bishop unknown to me: alcoholic, asthmatic, repressed cipher.
Where was the poet of "Sestina"? As if in search of B. Traven, I
turned not to the author but to the authority of the work itself.
I write for an imagined reader armed with *The Complete Poems,
1927–1979* and *The Collected Prose*, prepared to study and admire
the architecture of Bishop's world without unduly fussing over the
poet's inevitable human-ness.

This study focuses on Elizabeth Bishop's choice of rhetorical and
linguistic strategies in composing individual poems and stories, and
the larger thematic and aesthetic issues that knit her collections
together. Bishop's poetry attempts to attain a wholeness, like
Leaves of Grass or the "(W)hole of Harmonium" that Wallace
Stevens envisioned his *Collected Poems* to be. Her faith in, and
understanding of, the unifying aesthetic and social power of her
language-art is the topic of this study. While I draw upon biographical information and unpublished letters and journals, especially in
discussing work based on Bishop's childhood, I have chosen to
focus primarily on the poetry and published fiction. Bishop's journals and letters are engaging and indispensable, but the careful
composition and ordering of the five collections published in
her lifetime (*North and South*, *A Cold Spring*, *Questions of Travel*,
the first *Complete Poems*, and *Geography III*) point to her belief
in the aesthetic self-sufficiency of both her individual poems and
her tightly organized books. The autonomy of literary form may
be illusory or mystified, but Bishop subscribed wholeheartedly to
it. She did not, however, necessarily regard that form as totalizing,
and her attempt to mediate between autonomy and incompletion
constitutes one of the empowering motifs of her work.

The critic does not have to concur with the notion of aesthetic sufficiency, but Bishop's valorization of lyric form is a product of her essentially romantic faith in art, and requires full consideration. Further, though Bishop might not have acknowledged this, the letters and journals, as distinctly as the poems and stories, form identifiable literary entities; to excerpt from these to support arguments about the poems disregards the special qualities of their genres. Though like other critics I draw upon this material at times, I believe it does justice neither to the poems and fiction nor to the letters and journals to regard any of these texts as more or less autonomous in form, intent, or accomplishment than the others. While I have felt free to read the poems and stories intertextually, to read Bishop's entire body of work this way, with sufficient regard for her accomplishment in both fictional and autobiographical genres, would require a much larger study.

A common approach to Bishop's poetry argues that her sensibility was shaped in large part by her interest in the visual arts, particularly in the work of Klee, Ernst, and de Chirico. Bishop certainly held these artists in high regard, and undoubtedly she learned a great deal from them. Poetry, however, is made of language, and while the perceptions of visual artists may bear some analogy to the fictional approximation of visual perception in poetry, perception and imagination are not available to others except through the medium in which they are expressed. Perception is only an abstraction until embodied in a work of art, and in the practice of art the medium, not intention, perception, or imagination, is the primary shaping element. For poetry, the constraints of the social medium of language, and the tension between desire and possibility — a tension the reader perceives only in the actual performance of the poem — constitute the problematic in which the poem occurs. This study attempts to deal with this problematic, not because it is the only possible way to approach Bishop's poetry (clearly it is not), but because preceding book-length studies of Bishop have not sufficiently engaged the primary issues of Bishop's language and rhetoric.

Finally, this study resists certain tenets that were recently popular among feminists, tenets that would have been anathema to Bishop, not because she was unaware of the cultural and social issues of being a woman, but because she noted that segregating poets by gender invariably marginalized women. As an inheritor of the romantic faith in imagination, Bishop expected poetry (her own and others') to appeal to that perhaps nonexistent faculty rather than strictly to the sociopsychological construct the individual presents to the ordinary world. That imagination is a transcendent, nonlimiting power is what distinguishes it from the social and psychological views of human limitations most in favor now. It is puzzling, however, what anyone—feminist or otherwise—who subscribes to the notion of gender, race, ethnicity or religion as limiting factors finds of interest in any poetry, let alone poetry as transparent in its appeal to the transcendent imagination as Bishop's. Perhaps this is why some critics have had more to say about what they believe to be her sexuality than about her poetry.

From the viewpoint of the sociologist of literature the concept of the imagination may appear to be a manifestation of outdated bourgeois idealism. Although duly skeptical, however, and even critical of the relationship between the imagination and the phenomenal world, Bishop, like most poets of the modern era, explicitly believed in this now-suspect capability to transcend individual limitations. She was not very successful in empathizing with people of distinctly different ethnic or racial backgrounds, and the voices and personae derived from her observations of the inhabitants of Brazil, for example, are not always convincing or effective. However, this is a particular aesthetic failing, and does not negate the principle involved, which is Shakespearian, Keatsian, and at the very heart of the metaphor of creativity as Bishop understood it.

Because Bishop refused to privilege gender as a limitation (although some of her well-meaning readers did, as when Robert Lowell called her "our best woman poet, after Marianne Moore"), she resisted publishing her work in restrictive anthologies and journals and kept exposure of her private life to a minimum. It was not a lurid or especially exemplary life, but it did produce a good deal of childhood trauma, for reasons Bishop makes evident in some of her poems and stories, and her travels and years of expatriotism give her biography a conventionally romantic flavor. The number and depth of her friendships are remarkable, as her extensive, often brilliant letters testify. Her correspondences with May Swenson and Kit and Ilsa Barker, for example, would make lengthy, fascinating books in themselves. Her sexuality, which fascinates critics who would like to appropriate it (rather than her) for purposes of literary politics, was probably less exciting than these sexual colonialists would wish. The most interesting moment, probably, from the point of view of literary posterity, was the time Robert Lowell, visiting Bishop in Maine after his first divorce, nearly asked her to marry him. Bishop's intense fondness for Lowell survived this awkward interchange, fortunately, and her subsequent correspondence with him constitutes one of her richest works.

Bishop's poems and stories are highly personal, but they do not constitute a conventional autobiography. Instead, they recount the story of her attempts to invent a language adequate to her perception, and require a critical approach that acknowledges the primacy of that concern. Therefore, the critical works that have informed the present study are primarily those that deal with problems of language, imagination, perception, and rhetorical strategies. At least equally important are the poetry, journals, letters, and other prose by authors admired by Bishop. It is appropriate to list here some of those works — both critical and creative — since their influence is pervasive rather than local, and they inform a general approach rather than a specific method or argument. The literary works Bishop herself admired, consulted, and drew upon include Keats, *Letters* (the Rollins edition, which Bishop annotated), Coleridge, *Biographia Literaria*, and travel books such as Darwin, *Voyage of the Beagle*, William Bartram, *Travels*, Alfred Russel Wallace, *A Narrative of Travels on the Amazon and Rio Negro*, and Audubon, *Journals*. Along with the poetry of Herbert, Wordsworth, Frost, Auden, Eliot, and Lowell, these books are essential for readers of Bishop's work. The more contemporary works of critical theory that inform the present discussion include Alastair Fowler, *Kinds of Literature*, Raymond Williams, *The Country and the City*, Elaine Scarry, *The Body in Pain*, Michel Foucault, *The Archaeology of Knowledge*, Dominick LaCapra, *History & Criticism*, and Sharon Cameron, *Writing Nature* and *The Corporeal Self*.

Peterborough, N.H.   C.K.D.
August 1992

Acknowledgments

Finally, a decade after her death, Elizabeth Bishop is drawing the critical attention due a major poet. Though Bishop studies remain "raw" not "cooked," several works have served the poet, and successive generations of scholars, well. I am particularly indebted to Candace MacMahon for her pioneering bibliographical study; to Lloyd Schwartz and Sybil Estess for their suggestive collection, *Elizabeth Bishop and Her Art*; to Thomas Travisano and Robert Parker for their recent assessments of Bishop's topics and development; to the late David Kalstone for his eloquent biographical study, *Becoming a Poet*; to Lynn Keller for her suggestive assessment of Marianne Moore's influence on Bishop in *Re-making It New*. Two recent critical studies by Lorrie Goldensohn and Bonnie Costello appeared after I had completed this study, but nonetheless I have found their insights challenging and informative.

I have received ongoing scholarly assistance from Timothy Murray and his staff at the Olin Library, Washington University (Bishop-Swenson Correspondence); the curatorial staff at Houghton Library, Harvard University (Bishop-Lowell Correspondence as well as Bishop's personal library); Firestone Library, Princeton University (Bishop-Baker Correspondence). Special gratitude is due Mary Marks and her staff at Daniel Webster College for accepting my urgent appeals as routine.

Unlike many scholars, I owe my greatest debts not to grant agencies or institutional support but to several friends who kept me committed to this project over many difficult years. For his encouragement and trust, I want to thank A. Walton Litz who, from our first meeting at the Bread Loaf School of English, has displayed a generosity and wisdom rare in the cramped quarters of the academy; for his quiddity and his correspondence, I am indebted to Don Keck DuPree; for his insights into racial discourse in American poetry, I am grateful to Aldon Nielsen; for her belief in my project at a crucial time, I record my gratitude to the late May Swenson. And finally, for their encouragement and expertise, I thank Elizabeth Maguire and T. Susan Chang at Oxford University Press who smoothed every rough passage.

My greatest debts, I hope evident throughout this study, are to Elizabeth Bishop, especially for *Questions of Travel*, which kept me company and kept me sane in a parlous decade long ago, and to William Doreski, who not only showed me my first turtle but also made this study a reality.

Contents

A Note on References

Bracketed notations within the text or following quotations refer to Elizabeth Bishop's published volumes, abbreviated as follows:

North & South: NS
Poems: North & South — A Cold Spring: CS
Questions of Travel: QT
The Complete Poems: CP1
Geography III: G
The Complete Poems 1927–1979: CP
The Collected Prose: CPr

Although I identify in the course of discussion or in bracketed abbreviations the collections in which the poems originally appear, for the convenience of the reader I usually give page references to *The Complete Poems 1927–1979*, which is more readily available. All of Bishop's cited prose, except one uncollected review, is from the *Collected Prose*. References to other authors appear in notes following the text.

ELIZABETH BISHOP

All the untidy activity continues,
awful but cheerful.

"The Bight"

INTRODUCTION

The Restraints of Language

When Elizabeth Bishop exchanges *looks* for *visions* in "Poem" ("About the size of an old-style dollar bill . . ."), she renews a life-long commitment to a language of seemingly transparent simplicity, one that privileges the articulation of the experience of the senses instead of the interior world of the psyche or the romantic impulse toward epiphany and the world of the spirit. The tropes of Bishop's domestic, pastoral, or exotic landscapes serve knowledge only insofar as they cloak, while exteriorizing, the unspoken and inarticulate interior, refusing either to resolve or deconstruct the binary opposition. For some critics, this binding of experience in a restraining rhetoric, one that depersonalizes as it simplifies, has become a characteristically American manner. Certainly it distinguishes Bishop from Wordsworth, with his penchant for "spots of time," however superficially her work suggests his.

Bishop encloses her powerful tropes of travel, art, and loss in an elliptical rhetoric of aporia. Her appearance of simplicity depends upon a clarity of direct statement and a carefully delineated series of landscapes and dramatic situations. Words seem to stand for concrete entities and Emersonian "natural facts," conveying what William James would have called "verifiable" knowledge. She worried over poems through many years and drafts, hoping to detect and omit any revelation of personality. Her concern with the quotidian — the unadorned (though fictionalized) experience and travels of the poet — seeks its aesthetic tension not from the unusual

3

nature of her subject matter, nor from any profound conflict with traditions (she works extraordinarily well within lyric conventions — seeming to work with and against at the same time), but rather from the restraint imposed by language itself. What Robert Lowell saw as Bishop's "classical serenity" suggests the impressive control her language imposes on her subject matter, her resistance to abstraction, easy closure, and the mere illusion of plenitude in meaning.

In "At the Fishhouses," from her second book, *A Cold Spring*, the language, having gained a good deal of momentum, becomes increasingly sensuous and specific, and claims, at last, through the trope of the sea, a thoroughly sensate and utterly transparent climax that invites entry, immersion, and transference:

> If you should dip your hand in,
> your wrist would ache immediately,
> your bones would begin to ache and your hand would burn
> as if the water were a transmutation of fire
> that feeds on stones and burns with a dark gray flame.
> If you tasted it, it would first taste bitter,
> then briny, then surely burn your tongue.
> It is like what we imagine knowledge to be:
> dark, salt, clear, moving, utterly free,
> drawn from the cold hard mouth
> of the world, derived from the rocky breasts
> forever, flowing and drawn, and since
> our knowledge is historical, flowing, and flown.

[CP, 65–66]

As a descendent of Thoreau, Hawthorne, Melville, and Frost, and an antecedent of Susan Howe's New Englandly, noun-driven Language poetry, Bishop has been an (I)witness. Her account of a repeated phenomenon — "I have seen it over and over" — the indifferent seas slopping over and above the stony shore wholly recreates the implied experience, maintaining the illusion of witness by the seductive staging of the event.

First, the poet tempts her readers into the realm of possibility: "If you should dip your hand in, / your bones would. . . ." She then courts plausibility with the logic of sequence: If one takes the first step — immersion (earlier in the poem Bishop notes that she believes in "total immersion") — then one is primed for the tide of events that will surely follow. Her adherence to physical, sensate realities underscores her knowledge, and engenders belief. Though readers may not understand this experience, they feel it; they experience it. In this process of transference, the poet effaces herself by making the moment of perception the reader's own, demonstrating that "It is like what we imagine knowledge to be." What, then, does *it* refer to? The sea, the water, the tides? Asked to make this metaphysical leap from the physical and sensory knowledge of the sea to the epistemological sense of it, one straddles the yawning chasm between what humans can know — "dark, salt, clear, moving, utterly free" — and that which projects unmoored minds into the "historical, flowing, and flown." This educational disclosure is locked in the language, which reveals itself to be nonrepresentational after all, but a code. Here lies the unnerving power of the reticence that requires interpretation through recognition that language *is* experience. Like Thoreau's "johnswort spring[ing] from the same perennial root in this pasture," Bishop's slopping sea requires the sight of "infant eyes." Both flower and sea court an original relationship through an infant's expressionless impressions in hopes of rekindling that "visionary gleam."

Bishop employs this distinction between *looks* and *visions* of the mind's eye throughout her career. This differentiation indicates a complex interplay between knowledge and language. Intelligibility (the very language of communication) is forfeited as poet and reader alike gaze, preliterate, with infant sight. Visionary "infant sight," however, means knowledge without language. Critics have repeatedly argued that Bishop's world, like her fairy-godmother Marianne Moore's, is one of observations, that she is a keen-eyed descriptive poet. Yet, this superficial assessment obscures the way Bishop uses her descriptive language to critique the presumptions of epiphany, the illusion of plenitude in the sublime, the superficial and premature insights of the picturesque. In her poetic practice, she is a severe critic of the romantic poets, skeptical, in her way, as Frost.

One of the earliest examples of the strategy of clearly distinguishing between the gaze of plain sight and the interiority of vision (while respecting the power of each) occurs in "The Imaginary Iceberg," a poem strategically placed early in her first book *North & South*. Here Bishop's metaphor of imagination and reality plays

upon (what Dickinson claims to be) the power of icebergs to "itali-
cize the sea":

> We'd rather have the iceberg than the ship,
> although it meant the end of travel.

[CP, 4]

This idea of imaginary travels tempting the traveler to a willing
doom through the relinquishing of a language-world of tropes recurs in "Questions of Travel," the title poem of her third collection,
when travel-weary Bishop questions whether it would have been
better to have stayed at home than to have exhausted herself on
exotic otherness. Only the imaginative vision can tempt her to consider renouncing first-hand observation. "This is a scene a sailor'd
give his eyes for," she notes. The dramatic choice described in
"The Imaginary Iceberg" reassures because of its interiority — "This
iceberg cuts its facets from within." That is, the iceberg cannot
actually endanger the world of the ship because being imaginary it
is merely a trope, utterly nonrepresentational, though still aesthetically satisfying. Icebergs (at least the imaginary variety) are also as
essential to one's spiritual welfare as is the soul: "(both being made
from elements least visible)."

The poet, however, like her surrealistic Man-Moth, refuses to rely
on introspective visions alone; she, too, must make "[her] rare, although occasional, visits to the surface." The imaginative dream
world, especially for one immersed too long or too deeply in it, carries great peril, as "The Unbeliever" (from *North & South*) discovers:

> But he sleeps on the top of his mast
> with his eyes closed tight.
> The gull inquired into his dream,
> which was, "I must not fall.
> The spangled sea below wants me to fall.
> It is hard as diamonds; it wants to destroy us all."

[CP, 22]

This seems a deliberate recollection of Melville's "spangled sea calm
and cool" in "The Castaway" chapter of *Moby-Dick*.

The paradox of lethal knowledge dominates "Over 2000 Illus-
trations and a Complete Concordance," another poem from *A
Cold Spring*. After a journey through engravings and wanderings,
Bishop seems to turn to an empowering lyric moment:

—the dark ajar, the rocks breaking with light,
an undisturbed, unbreathing flame . . .

[CP, 58–59]

She has already argued, however, that whatever one's imaginative regret, human life is historically linear — "only connected by 'and' and 'and'." Steadily she withdraws the raw language of impressions, of uninterrupted retinal images, of infant / speechless sight and the privileging languages of analysis and abstract emotional expression, describing the resultant diminished, alienated world as "colorless, sparkless, freely fed on straw," a world depleted by the very ignorance of our attention. Paradoxically, Bishop suggests that inspiration stems from originary speechless witnessing, but concurs with Wordsworth that such preliterate, sensuous states must be relinquished in order to record such visions.

The struggle to find a language willing to accommodate the traveler's fluid, trope-empowered knowledge (even as it concealed her personality) defines Bishop's career. Bishop believes in articulate knowledge, that which can be formed and can contain, and then imply, without recourse to abstraction, the deftly framed mysteries. She sees a responsibility to order the chaos about her through a way of seeing, an angle of vision; she foils a cruel, chaotic age with form, order, and clarity. Like Dickinson she is a poet who requires circumference.

Throughout her career, Bishop distinguishes between that which offers itself for scrutiny and that "back, in the interior, / where we cannot see" ("Cape Breton"). *Questions of Travel* is alive with references to such visual witnessing: "Januaries, Nature greets with our eyes" ("Brazil, January 1, 1502"); "the crowded streams / . . . turning to waterfalls under our very eyes" ("Questions of Travel"); and concluding with "The Riverman" who needs:

a virgin mirror
no one's ever looked at,
that's never looked back at anyone,
to flash up the spirits' eyes
and help [him] recognize them.

[CP, 107]

The Riverman requires an original reflection, like the imaginative need for "infant sight," to realize the spirits; for only then can this mortal traveler confront the "spirits' eyes." This infant witnessing, however, can no more be articulated than the old Nativity; the spiritual exchange is only implied.

Bishop's final word on these infant visions may be found in *Geography III* in "The Moose." For here, infant vision returns the gaze. As a busload of Boston-bound travelers drifts southward, dozing and dreaming, a moose appears from the "impenetrable wood." The reaction of the passengers consists of childish, half-articulate expressions as they acknowledge an event beyond their usual powers of speech:

> "Sure are big creatures."
> "It's awful plain."
> "Look! It's a she!"

Bishop heightens the awe of this roadside encounter by having the moose return those exclamatory and visual "looks" with its own regard:

> Taking her time,
> she looks the bus over,
> grand, otherworldly.
> Why, why do we feel
> (we all feel) this sweet
> sensation of joy?
>
> [CP, 173]

The experience of the moose seems to complement that of the travelers.

Obviously these poems rest on more than chance encounter, random observation. Bishop's writings hinge upon the knowledge within the word, lying within the very surface of her poetry. She would surely assent to Wallace Stevens's view that "[Poetry] is an illumination of a surface, the movement of a self in the rock." Her poetic emerges from a writing governed by exposure through and by language in which knowledge itself requires reticence and control. Too often this poetic requirement has been translated into a psychological deficit in the poet. Many critics have seen Bishop as peculiarly reticent, personally repressed, or unhealthily self-effacing. They write of Bishop the solitary, the lesbian, the cipher, the helpless victim of the phallocracy trapped in the prisonhouse of gender. Even *T.V. Guide* (in its program blurb for "Voices and Visions") describes Bishop as that "shy, reticent poet (1911–1979) who produced works known for their precision and artistry."

The assertiveness of two of Bishop's formal masterpieces, "Sestina" and "One Art," belies this simplistic characterization. These poems bracket a collection of poetry tough enough to confront the awfulness (a favorite Bishop word) of life's inequities and pain without self-pity or self-indulgence, and with an epistemological skepticism rigorous as any philosopher's.

Much of *Questions of Travel* consists of a midcareer return to childhood modeled on Lowell's *Life Studies*. The prose story, "In the Village," prompts and to some degree empowers the poems of the "Elsewhere" section. While only three of that section's poems concern childhood, the dislocations and terror of the childhood shared in the story pervade that "Elsewhere." "Sestina" holds those preliterate years at arm's length, relying on the stark rigors of form and diction to convey while concealing the child's mysterious knowledge of the interior of the domestic world.

Unlike the earlier sestina, "A Miracle for Breakfast," this poem magically relaxes into its rigid form. So effortlessly does this childhood tableau conform to its form that Bishop feels compelled to change the title from the manuscript "Early Sorrow" to "Sestina," perhaps doubtful whether without so clear a signal readers would appreciate its virtuosity. The sequential repetition of the six end words—house, grandmother, child, stove, almanac, tears—draws the strength of variety from the unexpected sixth: tears. The poem's problem is to restrain the truth (that is, the intrusive personality) of this memory, heightening the revealed knowledge through an unobtrusive rhetoric of repetition.

"Sestina," from *Questions of Travel*, is nourished by the enduring emotional bond between the child and her grandmother. The forced selectivity of poetic form isolates and amplifies key elements in the comparatively diffuse prose memoirs (that is, "In the Village" and other fictionalized memoirs written and first published in the early 1950s). The arresting success of this poem, constructed from familiar memories, illustrates how crucial compactness is to Bishop's work. The insistent undercurrents of sadness and loss dominate the tone, but the Little Marvel Stove repeatedly chimes in with its cheerfully domestic sounds. Consequently, the dominant note of the poem, despite the undercurrents, is the moment of shared love, not loss. While the autumnal equinox signals an additional seasonal change for the grandmother, the simple declarative — "September rain falls on the house" — delineates a still but living moment.

Domestic activities, centered about the Little Marvel Stove, expend the energy that would otherwise be siphoned off by sorrow: "she cuts some bread . . . tidies up . . . puts more wood on the stove . . . busies herself about the stove . . . sings to the marvellous stove." The diction lifts the apprehensive solemnity of the scene while the rhythm sustains the intensity of the busy work. In her tidying the grandmother fastens the "clever almanac / on its string," perhaps to escape the foretold future. She fails, however, to skirt the prophetic spell, as the almanac hovers above them, causing a physiological response:

> She shivers and says she thinks the house
> feels chilly, and puts more wood in the stove.

> [CP, 123]

The ambiguity of that chill recurs often in Bishop's poetry: its significance ranges over the dampness of the day, the sorrows of a lifetime, the grandmother's awareness of her mortality, and her fears for the child's future well-being. Still, it fails to chill the warmth of the recalled moment.

The unnamed child inherits the final movement of "Sestina." Operating in a context of grief and loss, the child-artist nonetheless refuses to be engulfed by it. She prefers to frankly embrace it, drawing upon it as she begins the life-long process of constructing her world. The grandmother, who "tasted of tears," set the tone; the child perceives the emotion if not the source of the sorrow:

> . . . but the child
> is watching the teakettle's small hard tears
> dance like mad on the hot black stove . . .

> . . . Birdlike, the almanac
> hovers half open above the child,
> hovers above the old grandmother
> and her teacup full of dark brown tears.

The shared fate of the hovering almanac would be one of "small hard tears" and "dark brown tears" were it not for the monosyllabic and manic Terpsichorean challenge of "the hot black stove." The moment dominates the future foretold of the almanac.

The child's sensitivity and sensibility deserve an illustration, which she provides herself. The Marvel Stove and the almanac assume choral roles as they ominously set the stage: "*It was to be*, says the Marvel Stove. / *I know what I know*, says the almanac." The child presents her genre scene:

> With crayons the child draws a rigid house
> and a winding pathway. Then the child
> puts in a man with buttons like tears
> and shows it proudly to the grandmother.

In spite of the "rigid" formality of death, the stanza has authority and gusto. Whatever psychologists might read into the child's drawing, the child-artist has displaced the sorrow by making it ornamental, transforming it into a creation worthy of pride.

The correspondence between the catalogue of the grandmother's knowledge (the almanac) and the child's emotional graphic (her drawing) materializes in the final stanza. The almanac's "little moons" shed into "the flower bed the child / has carefully placed in the front of the house." Like the drawing this botanical arrangement relies upon artifice to unseat the misery of the context. The almanac's final injunction—"*Time to plant tears*"—suggests that this infusion of sorrow may infect the actual soil of the village, but what the tears will produce, as they grow, is beyond the province of the poem.

The envoy leaves the grandmother and child suspended in memory, the reader's and Bishop's. Each is forced to confront the unknown wonder, "the marvellous stove," "the inscrutable house." That Puritan literary descendent, the almanac, withholds its knowledge of the wonders of the invisible world as it dangles over them both. In the plain colloquial light of the word, objects in "Sestina" become the means of interpretation. The astonishment of the scene resides in the power of the stove—and the sestina—to hold the inhabitants of the poem suspended in that moment of recall, belief, and love.

Gramley Library
Salem College
Winston-Salem, NC 27108

Though Bishop evades loss in "Sestina," she confronts it in her masterful villanelle, "One Art," from *Geography III*:

> The art of losing isn't hard to master;
> so many things seem filled with the intent
> to be lost that their loss is no disaster.
>
> Lose something every day. Accept the fluster
> of lost door keys, the hour badly spent.
> The art of losing isn't hard to master.
>
> Then practice losing farther, losing faster:
> places, and names, and where it was you meant
> to travel. None of these will bring disaster.
>
> I lost my mother's watch. And look! my last, or
> next-to-last, of three loved houses went.
> The art of losing isn't hard to master.
>
> I lost two cities, lovely ones. And, vaster,
> some realms I owned, two rivers, a continent.
> I miss them, but it wasn't a disaster.
>
> —Even losing you (the joking voice, a gesture
> I love) I shan't have lied. It's evident
> the art of losing's not too hard to master
> though it may look like (*Write* it!) like disaster.
>
> [CP, 178]

The simple sentence of the opening stanza seems to subvert the title, declaring that this poem is *not* about art; rather, it is concerned with an acquired skill, the "art of losing." Critics anxious to commiserate with poets will find this reading psychologically appealing. Not only does it guarantee numerous opportunities to rehearse this art, but (Bishop suggests through the acceleration of enjambment) supplies materials branded "with the intent / to be lost." This perishable quality simultaneously allows for repeated practice and diminishment, if not extinction, of the pain. The poet offers a primer for the mastery of disaster, couched in the Puritan form of the sermon to others for their moral improvement.

Mindful always of the common auditor, Bishop forces the second stanza to visualize with the philosophical ruminations of the first. Readers learn precisely how to master this art, and are urged to practice, to make it into a virtuous habit: "Lose something every day." A further injunction counsels the reception and approval of that resulting disorder—the "fluster"—produced by haste, undue agitation. Loss, art, master, disaster—the lofty conceptual diction of the first stanza crumbles in the mockery of this near rhyme. The "lost door keys, the hour badly spent" become concrete entities and lost time. The refrain vulgarly collides with "fluster"—to master fluster?—in an uneasy rhyme casting the very tone of the poem into doubt.

Bishop enforces a progressively dynamic, almost uncontrollable, schedule of loss in the third stanza. *Then* simply shifts the focus to the next lesson. No longer does the homilist tally manageable, sympathetic incidents; the poem has moved beyond them to over-whelming concerns: places, names, and destinations. Each reader must supply concrete examples. The "intent" of the first stanza blossoms into the broader intentions of "where it was you meant / to travel" of the third stanza. Bishop continues to induce specific details from the reader as the pace and range grow. Soon drained of places, names, and travel plans, the reader must struggle to fill the lists. The muted refrain rings hollow as these clustered catego-ries of loss and faster/disaster cacophonize.

After the impersonal professorial tone, the abrupt introduction of the lyric *I* requires immediate reappraisal of all that comes be-fore this stanza. The homilist's experiential knowledge, suppressed in the first half of the poem, surfaces as the teacher has obviously experienced frustration in the auditor's ability to comprehend these lessons of loss. Bishop draws to the heart of the matter and sum-mons the ultimate parting gift, her mother's watch—an artifact that links the living and dead, recalling a time, expressing a genera-tion—making tangible the feeling of irretrievable loss. Bishop liter-ally lost her mother's time, as the stories "In the Village" and "Gwendolyn," and the poems "Sestina" and "Manners" all demon-strate. Looking beyond autobiography to the truth of this loss, however, Bishop exploits what is, after all, only one more "minor family relic."

The exemplum confounds conventional ideas of the subjective and objective, and demonstrates that loss is grave and universal, but too conventional to be deeply personal. She defers the threat of sentiment by the sweeping rhetorical gesture of "And look!" Her life, no longer a chaos of events, seems orderly and safe as Bishop inventories and schedules her losses: "my last, or / next-to-last, of three loved houses went." Her autobiography assumes an oddly reassuring linearity and predictability as the poem hurtles toward its closure. In spite of approximate knowledge — "my last, or next-to-last" — the end is palpable by its very proximity.

This registry of loss proceeds to the missing "three loved houses." Even that great modifier *loved* cannot convert these houses into homes. In spite of the wisdom of Bishop's crusade — "Home-made, home-made! But aren't we all?" (see "Crusoe in England") — the expatriot narrating this poem remains homeless.

The narrator, further emboldened by self-knowledge, begins again with "I lost." The scale has tipped; forsaking the personal for "two cities, lovely ones" the poet supplies lineaments and character to these scenic vagaries. Like the child-artist of "Sestina," the speaker approaches the unspecified, the unembraceable, yet concrete, type of loss: "two rivers, a continent," the loss of which suggest the impermanence, the unpossessable nature of the earth itself.

Though there remains a tension between the public and private exempla, that tension is ill-defined and ill-conceived. Bishop has adhered to the standards and expectations of her aesthetic; she has captured knowledge within the language and form of the villanelle. Yet with the displaced utterance delivered sotto voce, Bishop conveys a struggle between growing self-knowledge and her poetic of reticence in this dialogue between the self and the lost. "Even" moors this hierarchy of loss to that always poorly articulated world of extremity — without you, I can't go on, I can't live without you — those contracted conditionals meant to express the inexpressible love between two people. What threatens to emerge is that very thing her rhetoric strives to cloak: the self, naked to the vagaries of language. This ultimate series of I–You dependencies is the final protest against human perishability. Herein lies the true lesson of loss: "—Even losing you." Turning from her common audience, Bishop allows the parenthetically ensnared qualities to create a caesura: "(the joking voice, a gesture / I love)." Readers participate in the auditory and visual recall of pleasure (not pain) reduced to this synecdoche for the severed other. The positive qualities of this ultimate sacrifice displace the irritations and categorizations that came before in the poem. The situation challenges not the pupils but the master herself. In the almost processional resignation of "I shan't have lied. It's evident" rests the captive wisdom of the poem. In the extended refrain—

> the art of losing's not too hard to master
> though it may look like (*Write* it!) like disaster.

—readers see that parenthetical cure for the only true disaster. This encapsulated lesson is for the master alone; unlike the free, gestural "And look!" designed to deflect attention from the self, the parenthetical injunction maps a course for only one. The poet knows that only knowledge, not wisdom, can be shared. Like the child in "Sestina," the adult must also make some*thing* of absence. Her reward is the knowledge with which to write. In this rare command—"(*Write* it!)"—Bishop distinguishes herself from even Stevens's "Snow Man," who is "nothing himself," emerging as she does in this dramatic echo of William Carlos Williams's "Say It!"

The formal constraints of the sestina and villanelle freed Bishop to work with personal material without inducing the maudlin self-despairing tone she despised. The most forbidding and private sorrows, monumentalized in art, oddly affirm human dignity, emotion, and care. What follows is an examination of the buoyant heightened sophistication of Bishop's authority and artistry. This book does not seek, as some have, to demonstrate the poverty of her vision or her life. Rather it offers contexts and readings that emphasize the intelligence, resourcefulness, and grace with which Bishop's poetry mediates between rigorous aesthetic expectations and a skeptic's heartfelt search for the knowable.

CHAPTER 1

Deconstructing Images

Much that characterizes Elizabeth Bishop's writing—what Randall Jarrell called that "whole moral and physical atmosphere"—originates in her language of exteriority. Her assertive rhetoric of geographical situation encourages us to read her poems as maps, as documents that confirm the reader's sense of place and physical presence. Two-dimensional surfaces (maps, mirrors, paintings) preoccupy her because poetry shares both their limitations and possibilities, and because their problematic relationship to the actual world challenges ordinary definitions of fiction and fact. If Bishop seems a skilled cartographer, it is because her tropes of geography convince the reader of her knowledge of the world. Her charting of contours and elevations, summits, valleys, and seas embodies and extends the language of terrain and the evocative power of specific locale.

Because the language of exteriority is largely one of visual imagery, the problem of surface appearance dominates Bishop's writing. Though she works to engage all the senses in the "experience" of her poems, she turns most frequently to visual phenomena, or, like Keats in the Nightingale Ode, to the issue of visual deprivation. The phenomenal world, in her idealist argument, thrives or fails on the basis of our ability to see it rather than on the strength of its independent existence. This, however, is not a philosophical assertion but a linguistic one. The vocabulary of exemplary sight can focus the "things" of the world for closer examination and experience. From this reliance on the exemplary image and visual engagement, what John Ashbery has called Bishop's "thingness," the clarity of her writing derives. Critical appreciation of Bishop's world has focused on her "painter's eye," though it would be more appropriate to call it, oxymoronically, a painterly vocabulary and syntax.

Bishop's preoccupation with reflections, interfaces, and surfaces indicates her interest in the visual symptoms of presence rather than with transcendental immanence. She labors to momentarily affix those uneasy symptoms with a flexible syntax and a seemingly casual yet effective sense of structure. Unlike those mirrors or mirror images of transport (such as the mirror in *Through the Looking Glass*) and distortion (for instance the *Portrait* of Dorian Gray), the framed, fading surfaces described by her poems complete a self-portrait or a landscape (as in "The Gentleman of Shalott") or recall one (as in "Poem"), only to question its presence, permanence, or form. As the vocal perspectives shift through presentation and withdrawal, the voice reveals itself as distinct and personal rather than coolly objective, photographic. Her poems argue more about how the world seems than how it is, so their prospects are potential, not static, not subject to the mapmaker's art.

Mirror reflections, landscape inventories, paintings of people and places function less as subjects and more as central devices of Bishop's language-strategies. I turn to this body of work to determine how the use of such devices challenges the convention of *ut pictura poesis*. Her earliest "momentary surfaces" are mirrors and reflections. Of particular interest is how she distinguishes framed, vanishing images (as in mirrored reflections) from the expanding and contracting (perhaps even more threatening) reflections in water. On the other hand, her topographical inventories of land and sea (notably "Florida," "Questions of Travel," "Brazil, January 1, 1502," and "North Haven") build through a series of momentary aural sensations. Bishop depends upon successive images to recreate the experience of the place, as well as to mime the painterly effect of overlapping, merging imagery in poems like "Poem" ("About the size of an old-style dollar bill . . .") and "Large Bad Picture," which openly critique the aesthetic of painting. Though my discussion of the poet and the visual arts centers in these poems, it will also examine how the rhetoric of visual aesthetic functions mnemonically to control while unleashing the past. Finally I will show how "The Monument," a genuine *objet d'art* poem, defines its own strategic relationship to contemporaneous monument poems by Lowell and Berryman.

Natural surfaces, the raw stuff of geography, require a language that mediates between nature and culture and marks their intersections. The surface of Bishop's sea, for instance, like most romantic water views, conforms in verbal purpose to the larger rhetoric of the life cycle. Though not as ominous as the ocean of Marianne Moore's "A Grave," the description of the sea of "At the Fishhouses" conceals through metaphors of precious metal and stone as much as it reveals through its verbs of massive and meditative power:

> All is silver: the heavy surface of the sea,
> swelling slowly as if considering spilling over,
> is opaque, but the silver of the benches,
> the lobster pots, and masts, scattered
> among the wild jagged rocks,
> is of an apparent translucence
> like the small old buildings with an emerald moss
> growing on their shoreward walls.

[CP, 64]

The opaque but mirroring surface spills from sea to land, obscuring but transforming the shore world. This "mirror" offers no reassurance, no reflection of the meditating narrator. The shattered planes engender no correspondence between land and sea, and cannot function as a trope to link nature and culture. Instead, a counterresponse emerges unilaterally from the cold water. A rather incongruous döppelganger — the "curious," "interested" seal — exchanges "looks" with the poet. Like the exchange between the travelers and the moose, this marks a reflective self-confirmation. Without the penetrating presence of the seal, the sea would roll on without form, purpose, or direction:

> . . . The water seems suspended
> above the rounded gray and blue-gray stones.
> I have seen it over and over, the same sea, the same,
> slightly, indifferently swinging above the stones,
> icily free above the stones,
> above the stones and then the world.

The uneasy confirmation of self involves a risk of immersion, an affirmation of faith, an acknowledgment of the efficacy of the metaphor of creation. The seal breaking through the surface of the unknown initiates that which must be completed in experience.

Mirrors, rather than water, offer the most reliable, if most mundane, "silver" surfaces, and keep the poem more safely, if less adventurously, within the bounds of human culture. Bishop's self-reflections, however, even when confined in the mirror, assume a variety of forms and moods. In the playful symmetry of "The Gentleman of Shallot" [NS], Bishop departs from the mysteries of Tennyson's "Lady"—

> And moving thro' a mirror clear
> That hangs before her all the year,
> Shadows of the world appear

—and challenges the apparent fixity of perception, isolating that "sense of constant re-adjustment" that so often delights us. Here the mirror is intended to complete, not merely to reflect, this "gentleman" who is realized completely only through the glassy interface. He questions the likeliness of his apparent symmetry; he becomes half fiction. Verifiable truths and experiences succumb to a deliberately eccentric, Lewis Carroll–like humor. The glassy double exemplifies the candor of incompletion and undermines the possibility of self-reflexive understanding:

> He felt in modesty
> his person was
> half looking-glass,
> for why should he
> be doubled?
> The glass must stretch
> down his middle,
> or rather down the edge.

> [CP, 9]

The poem gestures toward the interior sources of reflections and edges. Denied any truly verifiable reality, the Gentleman considers simple resignation:

> . . . The uncertainty
> he says he
> finds exhilarating. He loves

that sense of constant re-adjustment.
He wishes to be quotes as saying at present:
"Half is enough."

The world cannot be all surface, and yet topography is a primary medium of exchange. The public half of the man revealed in the poem is only the purely sensate exterior. Rather than a narcissistic reflection—a direct confrontation of self-reflexivity—the poem generates a peripheral but convincing self-realization. The corporeal half not only completes the being but serves to sense and correct the fictive, fleeting self.

Reflective surfaces, although restricting sight, reassure by providing a means of self-inventory. As the childhood world depends upon the reader's relationship to things, the adult landscape requires a list or an inventory not only of the physical self, but also of the immediate landscape in which to situate the self. Even landscape inventories that do not acknowledge a contemplative presence in their itemizing, characterizing, and rescinding of various symptoms of presence offer the comfort of structure. Paralleling her oneiric interior scenes ("Paris, 7 A.M.," "Sleeping on the Ceiling," "Sleeping Standing Up") and her dockside census, "A Summer's Dream," these catalogues thrive on absence. Presentation and retraction seem simultaneous; the retreating landscapes mirror the lost world of deconstructing images recorded in such "momentary surfaces."

With unpopulated scenes, Bishop demonstrates a near-painterly restraint and regard for surface. The tropical, naturally baroque landscapes of Key West and Brazil lend themselves to this treatment. Like the self-generating fecundity of Theodore Roethke's "Root Cellar" where "[n]othing would give up life," these equatorial postcards bear tales of "fantastic fables and forms." Their regulation depends upon the poet's willingness to restrain and mold the outgrowth. "Florida" is the poem that proves the truth, or at least demonstrates the practicality, of Bishop's cartographic view.

The two peninsular stanzas of "Florida" [NS] move with certainty and mystery as Bishop imagines a Florida differing from that of Stevens and Crane. In doing so she depicts a state of death-in-life, a state of suffering for the lack of the chilly but bracing clarity and restraint of the north (see "First Death in Nova Scotia"), unanimated by human presence other than the poet's. To preserve the sensations around her through experience, the poet must follow the lines and life of the place.

The poem that will end in a babble of sound begins in the clarity of language. The poet's task is to name this world as if for the first time:

> The state with the prettiest name,
> the state that floats in brackish water,
> held together by mangrove roots
> that bear while living oysters in clusters,
> and when dead strew white swamps with skeletons,
> dotted as if bombarded, with green hummocks
> like ancient cannon-balls sprouting grass.
>
> [CP, 32]

The undergrowth, overcoming the instability of the landscape, secures the state for inspection. The relics of death and destruction cannot negate the surge of life heard in the syllables of the name or in the clustered life of the swamp. The connections the poem asserts—sound, suspension, cohesion, reproduction, depletion, growth—occur in terms of survival and persistence. Renewal becomes the essential characteristic of the scenery.

Applying language and scale to this world is a process of experiencing and humanizing it. As it is shaped by thumb and fingers, the peninsula takes on human dimensions. The sculpting, a nonverbal language-act, shapes a landscape of abundance, in which the plenitude of matter nearly overwhelms ordinary language. The excess of scene and action resists but finally yields to the imposition of human, renewable limits:

> The state full of long S-shaped birds, blue and white,
> and unseen hysterical birds who rush up the scale
> every time in a tantrum.
> Tanagers embarrassed by their flashiness,
> and pelicans whose delight it is to clown;
> who coast for fun on the strong tidal currents
> in and out among the mangrove islands
> and stand on the sand-bars drying their damp gold wings
> on sun-lit evenings.

By observing the preening and playing of these elemental creatures, Bishop characterizes as well as illustrates the place. Like the "scribbled hundreds of fine black birds / hanging in *n*'s in banks" of "Large Bad Picture," the images of this postcard strive to reverse the illusion of representation and embody the actual forms of language. In cartoon flashiness and technicolor excess, these tropical inhabitants blend into the highly artificial world of culture. At the same time, the inconsistencies and confusions of jungle life suggest the presence of the supernatural, a projection of the human world, in this swamp.

The outsized remains of the "enormous turtles, helpless and mild" (curiously more sympathetic than the indifferent teakettle tortoises of "Crusoe in England") suggest the pathos of mortality. The rounded empty sockets, "twice the size of a man's," delineate but withhold the final mysteries. Amid other anatomically and linguistically labeled debris, the skeletons form only one of many natural or artificial groupings:

> The palm trees clatter in the stiff breeze
> like the bills of the pelicans. The tropical rain comes down
> to freshen the tide-looped strings of fading shells:
> Job's Tear, the Chinese Alphabet, the scarce Junonia,
> parti-colored pectins and Ladies' Ears,
> arranged as on a gray rag of rotted calico,
> the buried Indian Princess's skirt;
> with these the monotonous, endless, sagging coast-line
> is delicately ornamented.

Such are the baroque ornaments of nature. The buried Princess gives expression to the surface, the rain-stirred shells freshen into art. Bishop's *clatter*, unlike Crane's *rustlings* in the palms, draws us not toward the visionary beyond but back to earth, to the "delicately ornamented" surface. The coastline is merely weighty and unremarkable in itself.

The first stanza, though barely suggesting the core of experience, prompts a consideration of the surface and sound of this state. However, the tropical setting inspires Bishop to an uncharacteristic and romantic gesture. She probes the surface in search of the essence itself. Rather than turning to the sea, the poet turns to the death-in-life world of the swamp in order to question the truth of

Emerson's "Circles" — "there are no fixtures in nature." Following
the descending buzzards, the narrative drifts toward extinction in
plenitude. The vaguely sinister imagery cannot diminish the oddly
reassuring *s* and *f* sounds:

> Thirty or more buzzards are drifting down, down, down,
> over something they have spotted in the swamp,
> in circles like stirred-up flakes of sediment
> sinking through water.
> Smoke from woods-fires filters fine blue solvents.

The confusion of elements in this passage combines with its soothing sounds to ease the reader's apprehension and promote some
natural (not celestial) correspondence between the land and sea,
air and fire, life and death. All motion becomes natural movement,
part of a continuum; perpetual change and renewal define the
beauty of the state. The Thoreauvian "disagreeables" in this setting
seem mere embellishments, immediately displaced by the more aesthetically appealing fireflies. They

> . . . map the heavens in the marsh
> until the moon rises.

The glowworms make a heaven of earth, but their poetic use depends on their ability to lead us downward into the marsh. The
telescoping images and sensations approximate the experience of
the fecundity of this exotic world.

Making an inventory diminishes the mystery and beauty of this
state. Straddling natural unpleasantness and heavenly abstractions,
Bishop occupies a middle ground:

> Cold white, not bright, the moonlight is coarse-meshed,
> and the careless, corrupt state is all black specks
> too far apart, and ugly whites; the poorest
> post-card of itself.

The heated intensity of the landscape vanishes in the reflected light,
the cold light of the moon. The dim, unfocused reflections engender an unnatural, unpleasant isolation. The scene, like a photograph, is improperly exposed. The tropics vanish in the night light.
Beyond the merely visible envelope of the landscape lies the actual
experience.

Unable to descend into a Stevensian "arranging, deepening, enchanting night," Bishop settles for the mysterious and worldly:

> After dark, the pools seem to have slipped away.
> The alligator, who has five distinct calls:
> friendliness, love, mating, war, and a warning—
> whimpers and speaks in the throat
> of the Indian Princess.

The harshly lit overexposures yield to interiority. This illuminated yet nocturnal creeping toward interior truths, like the savage attempts to penetrate the "hanging fabric" of the Brazilian jungle, links the experiential world with whatever lies in the unseen center of the landscape. The reptilian messenger is the incarnation of the sensations of the poem. The reproductive, unchecked urges of the "state with the prettiest name" become personified, oddly enough, through the character of the alligator. Though suggesting the possibility of communication, Bishop keeps utterances "buried" with the Indian Princess.

The shifting landmarks of this scenery occasion continual readjustment of points of view. The long, paired stanzas fail to isolate the particulars, but rather break between the experiential and imaginative truths. Unwilling to drift into Stevens's embellishing night, Bishop nonetheless finds satisfaction in the suggestion of "ghostlier demarcations, keener sounds."

The world explored by historical and contemporary tourist alike in "Brazil, January 1, 1502" and "Questions of Travel" [both from QT] consists of a similar progression of yielding images and fading sound. The "embroidered" and "tapestried" qualities of the landscape testify to gross overabundance. As Bishop characterizes and itemizes, she directs and colors the very experience of the poem. The piratical romance of "Florida" turns into the hellish fallen world of the conquistador in "Brazil, January 1, 1502," which in turn collapses into the fallen dream world of the unknowledgeable traveler in "Questions of Travel." Only this final voice asks questions of us. Yet the innocence of this voice is but one more pose of this skilled teacher. The gestures toward home, coupled with the dash-displaced queries and qualifications force us to share in the speculation and re-evaluation. In "The Monument" the shifting stance becomes a central strategy in Bishop's work.

The isolation of life and ornamentation in this tropical under-growth appeals to the need for experience. Florida becomes an actual state of mind when Bishop compresses the landscape into a glottal click in the throat of a solitary lizard. Everything shares in a single life. Vegetable and animal more than co-exist, they converge in the ongoing creation of this strange world. The overlapping images confirm the tourist's evidence. The projected response to the alligator's whimper demonstrates the comprehensiveness of the experience in the poem.

Most typically, the openness of Bishop's poems of visual clarity derives from the fiction of the objective stance. The experienced traveler, invoking the trope of geography as knowledge, returns to educate the uninitiated in the arts of perception. The final stanza of "Over 2,000 Illustrations" [CS] demonstrates the relationship of witness to reader, teacher, and student. After drifting between the "serious, engravable" imaginary journey and her actual travels, Bishop confronts her need to exfoliate and then dismiss these tropes:

> Everything only connected by "and" and "and."
> Open the book. (The gilt rubs off the edges
> of the pages and pollinates the fingertips.)
> Open the heavy book. Why couldn't we have seen
> this old Nativity while we were at it?
>
> [CP, 58]

All seems to bear God's fingerprints in this Blakean fallen world of "gilt" and complicity. Forced to reach beyond visual participation, the poem must assume the verbal weight of this "heavy" text, and in doing so become heavier itself. In this intertextuality, literary works merge in analogue with the mutuality of painterly forms. Yet whatever this act of influence generates fails to take palpable form, and the poem frames a canvas that gradually grows impoverished in our gaze:

> —the dark ajar, the rocks breaking with light,
> an undisturbed, unbreathing flame,
> colorless, sparkless, freely fed on straw,
> and, lulled within, a family with pets,
> —and looked and looked our infant sight away.
>
> [CP, 58–59]

Through the chink, we expect a self-illuminated scene, but witness instead what appears to be a self-consuming painting, which invites us to drift, with ineffective illumination, to the limits of perceptual experience. The poem occupies a Paterian interval, a momentary stay until "our place knows us no more." The construction and almost simultaneous suspension of this assembled world situates us in strange yet comforting places.

Though in these works of landscape and reflection Bishop employs a language that mimes and enlarges upon painterly techniques, she describes actual canvases in a somewhat different way. Reflections and inventories combine in family paintings and portraits to serve as mnemonics, keys to the recalling of childhood situations and relations. The agent of recall in "Memories of Uncle Neddy" (published in *The Southern Review*, 1977, but uncollected in Bishop's lifetime) and "Poem" is the same "minor family relic," a painting. "Memories" departs from the earlier expressionistic impressions of childhood. Gone is the horror of isolation, the distorted reflections of the village; these are replaced by an armchair amiability, a conversational tone. The hemispheric divisions of a life collapse as the chill of Nova Scotia dissipates in Rio. A family portrait of Uncle Edward occasions the recollections:

> [N]ot as he was, or not as I knew him . . . [but] before he became an uncle, before he became a lover, husband, father or grandfather, a tinsmith, a drunkard, or famous fly-fisherman — any of the various things he turned out to be.
>
> [CPr, 228]

Obscurity threatens the portrait in the form of the ever-encroaching mildew. Another kind of shadow threatened Uncle Neddy in life: "He looked already quite dead then, dead and covered with shadow, like the mold, as if the years of life had finally determined to obscure him." The narrator's preservation and positioning of the portrait momentarily lifts the shadows from the canvas and the past.

Canvassing life from a painting serves Bishop well in the early poem, "Large Bad Picture." Like many of the other poems in *North & South*, this poem-painting draws a place and time, an unpopulated landscape of the actual past. Sketching the remembered "Straight of Belle Isle or / some northerly harbor of Labrador," she preserves the vista; yet the great-uncle-school-teacher-

painter remains a cipher. Bishop learned from this strategy of linking ancestral memories to painting, and returned to it in the highly
refined "Poem" ("About the size of an old-style dollar bill . . ."),
in which a miniature painting releases the final wave of memories.
The Little Marvel Stove, the rocking chair, the many dolls, the
crazy quilt are displaced by

> —this little painting (a sketch for a larger one?) . . .
> Useless and free, it has spent seventy years
> as a minor family relic
> handed along collaterally to owners
> who looked at it sometimes, or didn't bother to.
>
> [CP, 176]

This is a poem of discovery, of acknowledgment that the world
Bishop crystallized in poetry and prose inspired graphic representation and deserves whatever preservation the ambiguous status of
art offers. The village takes shape as Bishop's syntax mimes the
ability of brushstrokes, shapeless in themselves, to build recognizable colored forms:

> It must be Nova Scotia; only there
> does one see gabled wooden houses
> painted that awful shade of brown.

The particulars—"tiny cows, / two brushstrokes each, but confi-
dently cows / . . . Up closer, a wild iris") yield to the shared sense
of "cold, early spring." The trope of recognition generates the exclamation, "Heavens, I recognize the place, I know it!" Barn, Pres-
byterian church, cows, and geese all bear the subscript, "I have
seen it."

A hesitant, conversational interlude links the genesis of this "inspirational" relic to its genealogy, serving as prelude to the final
exposition, the reconciliation. Bishop reflects on the freakish coin-
cidence of a vision shared with one she never knew, who like those
"particular geese and cows / [was] naturally before my time":

> Our visions coincided—"visions" is
> too serious a word—our looks, two looks:
> art "copying from life" and life itself,
> life and the memory of it so compressed
> they've turned into each other. Which is which?
> Life and the memory of it cramped,

> dim, on a piece of Bristol board,
> dim, but how live, how touching in detail
> —the little that we get for free,
> the little of our earthly trust . . .

[CP, 177]

This reduction of *vision* to *looks* characterizes Bishop as one in spirit with her "civilized" Crusoe when he questioned the value of his artifacts. Here Bishop provides her memory-manifesto: "art 'copying from life.'" This is the key to her coincidental visions and "unexpected moments of empathy." From the singular particularities of her life she constructs associative motifs that strike a human chord.

In "The Monument," [NS] Bishop's most static *objet d'art*, the poet looks finally at that which fails to return a gaze or respond to her inquiries. Unlike Berryman's staring statue ("Boston Common") or Lowell's commemorative elegy ("For the Union Dead"), "The Monument" stands not as memorial tribute but as speculation on a presence. This assemblage lacks recognizable form or significance; it is abstract art. From it the poet (and, by extension, the reader) must make something of it. The test is a perceptual one. The speaker guides her companion through a maze of possible viewpoints and stances. The voices of the poem (the patient, restrained narrator and her erratic, foolish companion) demonstrate Bishop's concern for experiential appreciation.

The title confers "significance." With the querulous first line, the narrator places her companion and the reader in a direct relationship to the poem's subject:

> Now can you see the monument? It is of wood
> built somewhat like a box. No. Built
> like several boxes in descending sizes
> one above the other.
> Each is turned half-way round so that
> its corners point toward the sides
> of the one below and the angles alternate.

[CP, 23]

Surface conforms to shape as the self-correcting lines present and clarify. As the box is realized, so must its spatial dimensions—its angles and bulk — be felt. The texture and artistic embellishments — "a sort of fleur-de-lys of weathered wood" — brand the sculpture as homely but enduring. The ironic characterization of the decoration as "ecclesiastical" suggests a comical spiritual dimension. Poet and reader can invest this structure with meaning. Bishop's similes play upon the associative qualities of landscape itself, creating an analogue between linguistic and psychological association. The "thin, warped poles" could be "fishing" or "flag" poles; the point is that they compel recognition through a logic of association that inheres in both the language of the poem and the psychology of the reader. In the fiction of the poem, companion and reader function at eye-level, where they are required to scan the landscape from sky to ground. The monument then sculpts itself by conforming to numerous similes, assuming the characteristics of each of them despite their variety.

The structure requires a context, so Bishop places it on a plane, situating the land and sea about it:

> The monument is one-third set against
> a sea; two-thirds against a sky.
> The view is geared
> (that is, the view's perspective)
> so low there is no "far away,"
> and we are far away within the view.

In order to place the tower spatially, Bishop sacrifices its third-dimension. The monument turns into a Max Ernst *frottage* with "splintery sunlight and long-fibered clouds." The entire scene — structure and setting — is a work of linear perspective and surface texture.

The opening question, "Now can you see the monument?", suggests an uninitiated presence. The realization of the monument's substantiality through description has remained unchallenged, but an unexpected and idiotic voice throws that substantiality into question:

> "Why does that strange sea make no sound?
> Is it because we're far away?
> Where are we? Are we in Asia Minor,
> or in Mongolia?"

All that descriptive realization is wasted; the point is missed. The companion's expectations fail to coincide with the actuality of the situation or the needs of the narrator.

This narrator now invokes imaginative "vaster realms," similar to the engraved scenes in "Over 2,000 Illustrations," hoping to engage the companion's sensibilities, if not her sympathy:

> An ancient promontory,
> an ancient principality whose artist-prince
> might have wanted to build a monument
> to mark a tomb or boundary, or make
> a melancholy or romantic scene of it . . .

[CP, 24]

The paired *a*s and *p*s create an integral associative chain—"ancient promontory," "ancient principality," "artist prince." The prince cannot help but seem a product of his prospect and place.

Yet the artist's imaginative appeal collapses under the weight of the companion's interpretation:

> "But that queer sea looks made of wood,
> half-shining, like a driftwood sea.
> And the sky looks wooden, grained with cloud.
> It's like a stage-set; it is all so flat!
> Those clouds are full of glistening splinters!
> What is that?"

Unaccustomed to experiencing art, the companion cannot accept the artist's imagination or invest the surface with her own.

The narrator returns to the thing itself: "It is the monument." Perhaps she hopes this definition would suffice by calling upon some consciousness of public statuary. The companion interrupts with one more unknowing assessment:

> "It's piled-up boxes,
> outlined with shoddy fret-work, half-fallen off,
> cracked and unpainted. It looks old."

The immediate rejection suggests disbelief. This spectator cannot see beyond the monument's exterior irregularities, the most mundane level of appearance.

The natural world is brought to bear on the surface; the elements speak:

> — The strong sunlight, the wind from the sea,
> all the conditions of its existence,
> may have flaked off the paint, if ever it was painted,
> and made it homelier than it was.

Although unable to resist change completely, the monument itself survives ordinary natural forces. Its artistic, man-made embellishments may disappear, but the structure is tougher than its surface.

The companion cannot withstand the monument's environment and grows disconsolate and disgruntled:

> "Why did you bring me here to see it?
> A temple of crates in cramped and crated scenery,
> what can it prove?
> I am tired of breathing this eroded air,
> this dryness in which the monument is cracking."

The unwilling onlooker succumbs to the eroding elements long before the mysterious structure does. The fatigue and frustration prompted by the incomprehensible defeats the companion, and she vanishes from the poem.

Like the world-weary Crusoe or the speaker of "Santarém," the narrator despairs of communicating aesthetic or emotional values. She finally resolves to review the structure and substance of the monument in the hopes of positioning us in relation to her experience:

> It is an artifact
> of wood. Wood holds together better
> than sea or cloud or sand could by itself,
> much better than real sea or sand or cloud.
> It chose that way to grow and not to move.

Bishop's monument resembles Stevens's nature-displacing vessel in "Anecdote of a Jar," which "took dominion everywhere."

As artifacts, these objects (jar, monument), by drawing upon the resources of culture, dominate the natural world. Both Bishop and Stevens suggest that such arbitrary creations claim a certain invulnerability. The works seem immortal, oddly organic, and entirely self-contained. Such observations, however, fail to address the subject's "thingness," its life as an object:

> The monument's an object, yet those decorations,
> carelessly nailed, looking like nothing at all,
> give it away as having life, and wishing;
> wanting to be a monument, to cherish something.
> The crudest scroll-work says "commemorate,"
> while once each day the light goes around it
> like a prowling animal,
> or the rain falls on it, or the wind blows into it.
> It may be solid, it may be hollow.

With the ambiguous metamorphic status of an organism, the monument has a taming and possessive effect equal to that of Stevens's jar ("The wilderness rose up to it, / And sprawled around, no longer wild"); it possesses the spirit of thingness: "wanting to be a monument, to cherish something." The very scroll-work functions as a primitive mnemonic, but what it calls to mind defies interpretation.

The interior remains unknown: "It may be solid, may be hollow." The mention of the inner state prompts further discussion:

> The bones of the artist-prince may be inside
> or far away on even drier soil.
> But roughly but adequately it can shelter
> what is within (which after all
> cannot have been intended to be seen).
> It is the beginning of a painting,
> a piece of sculpture, or poem, or monument,
> and all of wood. Watch it closely.

The prince of intentions returns as the potentially imaginative core or seed of this thing. The suggestion of a relatively dry and adequate interior confirms suspicions that the narrator has attained some interior knowledge through contemplating and attempting to explain this object's exterior. Bishop confirms that such sources as the monument's interior "cannot have been intended to be seen." The parenthetical reminder reiterates her common-sense and yet idealist aesthetic, which mediates between possibility and utility. The "beginning" is the source of imaginative experience for artist and audience alike.

Invoking "momentary surfaces" through a sensate vocabulary, these poems constitute a critical aesthetic of the perceptible world. Simultaneously appearing and fading scenes destabilize the fixed image, challenge the relationship of language to the senses, and confirm the complexity with which interior and exterior worlds mingle. These unstable reflections and peripheral visions embody the instability of even surface knowledge, yet offer a fuller sense of the interplay of language and experience. Although these poems resist the epiphanic grasp of immanence they offer a knowledge no less profound for their allegiance to a language of geography, landscape, and visual experience.

CHAPTER 2

Romantic Rhetorics

Epiphany and the power of naming (which in the modern era begins by naming the writer-as-authority) are two characteristically romantic-modern rhetorical embodiments of knowledge. Bishop, who largely learned these devices from Wordsworth, manipulates their conventions for some of her richest effects, and also for some of her most intriguing complexities. As I have previously argued, resistance to language that attempts to delve into the psyche or the world of the spirit characterizes her poetry. The process of resistance itself, however, constitutes a powerful rhetorical structure that shapes much of her best work. The epiphanic mode, which this chapter will discuss first, requires the poet to transgress the text and explicitly share its self-realization, its transcendence of language into immanence. Trust in the epiphany did not come readily to Elizabeth Bishop. As her poem "Santarém" warns, there is always the chance that the auditor might misunderstand the significance of the triggering subject and query "What's that ugly thing?", inadvertently mocking the ideational. What some critics consider Bishop's extreme reticence and excessive decorum may be linked to her notions of decency and communion, and to her ultimate distrust of epiphany.

The challenge for Bishop was to use epiphanic staging (the means of preparing the reader) without violating her aesthetic of reticence (a literary more than psychological tic). Though often labeled epiphanies by her critics, Bishop's gestures toward the Wordsworthian landscape of divine immanence do not usually function as such. In her encounters with the notion of a spiritual dimension suggested or revealed by landscape, the characteristic motion of her poems is a recoil from the beyond, retreating back into the poem itself.

This suggests the true depth of reticence in Bishop's poetic. Epiphany would and should open up the poem to uncontrollable exterior forces, relinquishing the law of metaphor and imposing a dimension beyond the ordinary reach of language. Bishop, who viewed poetry as a limited, and fortuitously limiting, exchange, refused to acknowledge any pressure to contain, expand, define, or even escape life through art. From the shark-filled "spangled sea" of "The Unbeliever" to the sheltered interior of "The Monument," from the road-checked interior of "Cape Breton" to the "armored cars of dreams" in "Sleeping Standing Up," Bishop clearly defines the terms of commerce in part by delineating the interiority and the exteriority of, respectively, her presence and the poem's surface strategies. Bishop's decorum surely included a sense of propriety or decency. Rather than a personality quirk, deficient ego, or exaggerated morality, however, her reticence informs her original language and diction, and is the basis of her refusal of many conventional poetic motifs that would, if allowed to, render her poems almost ordinary.

Throughout her work Bishop explores various rhetorical postures that respond to Wordsworth's epiphanic stance. At times she presents us with a natural vantage point, nature without human intervention. In "The Sandpiper" [QT], a creature scurries about in the midst of chaos; though "focused" and "preoccupied" he is not yet engulfed by the natural forces swirling about him. Unconscious of the threatening vastness, which humans might identify as epiphanic, he has developed a unique shoreline philosophy:

> The roaring alongside he takes for granted,
> and that every so often the world is bound to shake.

> [CP, 131]

At once a student of Blake ("in a state of controlled panic") and Keats ("The world is a mist. And then the world is / minute and vast and clear"), the shorebird sees his random fate as one with the minute particulars of the "millions of grains" of sand. In his element, the sandpiper knows none of the frustrating dislocations of humans in the landscape and therefore sees no need to transcend them. The traveler-spectator Bishop, on the other hand, needs to correct and interpret, as well as frame the scene:

> He runs, he runs straight through it, watching his toes.
>
> — Watching, rather, the spaces of sand between them,
> where (no detail too small) the Atlantic drains
> rapidly backwards and downwards.

Jealous of the bird's complete concentration on the particular, the poet introduces a human measure of scale. After all, the bird is obsessed with the sand, not his toes. Unlike the fleeing creatures of "The Armadillo" [QT], the sandpiper runs in a world devoid of human presence and its attendant scale. The poem shares a view from above — or beyond — this obsessed bird's seascape.

Though usually occupying a contemplative or a migratory presence in the landscape, Bishop occasionally assumes the advocacy-role of witness of human destruction of nature, the world of damaged shores. Exiled by her refusal of ordinary empathy, the poet grieves from a distance, regretting her undeniable kinship with destroyers. "The Armadillo" and "Brazil, January 1, 1502" confront the violent presence of humans in the natural world. Both deal with the role of Christianity in a fallen world in which humankind is a deadly presence. Bishop sees humans as oppositional, the only creatures capable of losing innocence. She traces sin to religion's door, accusing Christianity of sanctioning, or worse, ignoring true sin.

The paired Brazil poems shuttle back and forth through time, refusing epiphany through shifts in tone and regressions into history. In "Brazil, January 1, 1502" [QT], even as Bishop forsakes the literal for the pictorial frame, she identifies her intrusive presence in Brazil with that of the sixteenth-century conquistadors who, like herself, "left home." Perhaps like the wanderer of "Questions of Travel," these explorers "[t]hink of the long trip home." These men, unlike the poet, came to conquer, not to contemplate, and see their faith as the guiding spirit of their savagery. Leaving Mass, their celebration of interiority, the soldiers are heard

. . . humming perhaps
L'Homme armé or some such tune,
they ripped away into the hanging fabric,
each out to catch an Indian for himself —

[CP, 92]

Yet Bishop refuses to acknowledge their conquest, preferring instead to depict the ever-receding unknown of the tropical "hanging fabric." The hellish pollution of the second stanza clearly emanates from these "hard as nails" Christians. This perception becomes the opportunity to capitalize upon Keats's mistake:

Or like stout Cortez when with eagle eyes
He star'd at the Pacific — and all his men
Look'd at each other with wild surmise —
Silent, upon a peak in Darien.

"On First Looking into Chapman's Homer"

Cortez (unlike Balboa, the true discoverer of the Pacific) leads the assaulting Christians of Bishop's poem. Christianity here is part of that life "of wealth and luxury" that has brought death and destruction upon the meek. The voices of the vulnerable, miniature women mingle with the cries of the natural creatures of the interior world; they seek a protection in that world beyond humanity.

Escape into that world is not always possible, however, and epiphany may offer only the illusion of escape into another dimension. Within a few pages, Bishop returns to the unyielding persistence of human violence. Again Christianity, or the fragments of religious celebration, hovers in the background, sanctioning the disarray and cruelties of the piece. Unlike the protective fabric of the earlier poem, the firelit landscape of "The Armadillo" offers no sanctuary for the beleaguered creatures. The poem offers a glimpse of a secularized religious celebration, long since stripped of intent and meaning; the "frail, illegal fire balloons" ascend toward a waiting saint. In ascendancy, the fire floats assume lives of their own:

the paper chambers flush and fill with light
that comes and goes, like hearts.

[CP, 103]

Unstable and undirected, these heaven-bound balloons, gestures of "love," bear the potential of either love or war:

> Once up against the sky it's hard
> to tell them from the stars —
> planets, that is — the tinted ones:
> Venus going down, or Mars . . .

Oscillating between the heavenly extremes, the "tributes" represent a kind of chaos, not order; terror, not relief and penance. Bishop suggests that their very uncertainty — "With a wind, / they flare and falter, wobble and toss" — aggravates earthly insecurities. Inappropriate celebrations, which are both blasphemous and ignorant, violate the sacredness of ritual and disrupt the relationship between culture and nature. Such violation is likely to provoke fate and turn "dangerous":

> but if it's still they steer between
> the kite sticks of the Southern Cross,
>
> receding, dwindling, solemnly
> and steadily forsaking us,
> or, in the downdraft from a peak,
> suddenly turning dangerous.

The final line plummets toward the grim consequence of a moment of particularized sensation — an actual event, not merely a condition. Yet Bishop turns this tale of fragile faith and false tribute not on the plight of humanity but of innocent creatures. As messily careless in descent as ascent, the fire balloon "splatter[s] like an egg of fire," immolating airborne and ground-dwelling inhabitants alike. The scene commands full attention as the fire "egg" ironically brings death to the owl's nest:

> The flame ran down. We saw the pair
>
> of owls who nest there flying up
> and up, their whirling black-and-white
> stained bright pink underneath, until
> they shrieked up out of sight.

The appearance of the visibly immature ("short-eared") baby rabbit captures the instantaneous transition of the setting:

So soft! — a handful of intangible ash
with fixed ignited eyes.

Even as the poem reaches for the airy substance of the hare it
disintegrates into the elements, returning the speaker's gaze with
the steadfast certainty of death. An epiphany would reach for comfort and assurance, for insight and explanations through a glimpse
of a dimension in which suffering doesn't occur. The lyric hero,
however, responds only to ignorance and fear. In the italicized
exclamation of the closure, the poet challenges even the aesthetic
posture of poetry; she cries out as one forever earthbound:

> *Too pretty, dreamlike mimicry!*
> *O falling fire and piercing cry*
> *and panic, and a weak mailed fist*
> *clenched ignorant against the sky!*

The harsh deformations reject all falsification and softening of
reality. Invocation and resignation collapse together in an impotent
outcry as rage displaces epiphany. Unable to transcend the horror
of this awesome occurrence, yet unwilling to return into the experience of the poem, Bishop gestures angrily but agnostically toward
the beyond, challenging the type and substance of the incomprehensible. Bishop, like Wordsworth, sees humanity's dilemma as
one of estrangement from natural vision; but unlike her predeces-
sor, she has neither the ability nor the will to penetrate the otherworld and confirm herself in epiphany, further distancing herself
from such harsh realities. She can neither accuse nor ignore her
own kind; she can only grieve.

In her distrust of epiphany Bishop, however, occasionally finds
herself competing with and antagonistic toward the natural or phenomenal world, and that dramatic situation requires an epiphany.
"The Fish" [NS], Bishop's most frequently anthologized poem, relies upon a Wordsworthian spiritual exercise to justify a rowboat
transformation from plunderer to benefactor. The collapse of distinctions between land and sea, the air and earth of the speaker,
obscures the borders between life and art. Bishop perceives the
fish in land-language of "feathers" and "peonies" and "tinfoil" and
"isinglass." Even as she works those changes, however, the fish
works reciprocal wonders of its own. Passive resistance deprives

the fishing poet of her triumph: "He didn't fight. / He hadn't fought at all." She soon understands that her knowledge of the fish is inaccurate.

Evidence of past encounters—"two heavier lines, / and a fine black thread / still crimped from the strain and snap / when it broke and he got away"—tells of a different fish. Earlier seen as "battered and venerable / and homely" (the line-break softening the accuracy of description), the fish now assumes the mock-role of tribal elder and hero:

> Like medals with their ribbons
> frayed and wavering,
> a five-haired beard of wisdom
> trailing from his aching jaw.

[CP, 43]

Deprived of the fight, the poet must contemplate her position as the harbinger of death. The "little rented boat" marks a closed world wherein the speaker represents the moral force of her species. Taken by the incongruity and insignificance of the colloquy, the reader is swept from the sensuous into the psychological, then moved beyond earthly particulars to a spiritual whole:

> I stared and stared
> and victory filled up
> the little rented boat,
> from the pool of bilge
> where oil had spread a rainbow
> around the rusted engine
> to the bailer rusted orange,
> the sun-cracked thwarts,
> the oarlocks on their strings,
> the gunnels—until everything
> was rainbow, rainbow, rainbow!
> And I let the fish go.

As in the Christian parable, the oil upon the waters brings peace. It also engenders communication with the otherworldly. Through a rare Wordsworthian "spot of time," a genuine epiphany, the poet admits, somewhat reluctantly, a momentary conventional wisdom. This leap from perception to wisdom signals the arbitrariness so characteristic of the epiphany.

Though "The Fish" is certainly central to her canon, Bishop's boredom and dissatisfaction with the poem suggests a fear that the poem settles into sentiment instead of expanding into true wisdom. The matter-of-fact weightiness of the fish, a real survivor, lured the poet beyond the limits of her usual work, and tempted her out of her characteristic reticence. Fully aware and thoroughly suspicious of the technique and purpose of epiphany, Bishop usually contents herself with a suggestive advance toward and a sly retreat from the world of imaginative fulfillment beyond the page. Most of her journeys circumvent the critical moment of epiphany. Even as the poem reaches a crescendo, the poet reverses the flow, forcing it back into the journey, back within the intended limits of the poem itself. As "At the Fishhouses" demonstrates, Bishop is capable of presenting a Wordsworthian landscape only to carve the mass into her own figure. The glistening eternal present yields to the recurring past participles and tide of subjunctives that transform an otherworldly scene into a shared earthly experience— bounded by knowledge that is "historical, flowing, and flown."

The most useful examples of Bishop's near-epiphanic mode are found in her journey poems. Her destined or indifferent traveler sets forth with an unvoiced program, an inescapable linearity, but remains uncertain of the destination. The poems never lack a sense of discovery, though the end looms invariably in sight. "Cape Breton," "The Riverman," and "The Moose" suggest that Bishop was always aware of figures in the landscape; the problem was to present them without invoking a facile sentimentality that would accrue through gratuitous access to epiphany.

An opportunity to read the landscape for significance without plunging into epiphany comes in "Cape Breton" [CS], which challenges the preconceptions and sensitivities of the reader as it prepares, shapes, and withdraws a glimpse of the otherworldly. Bishop expects her readers to recall the lessons of its neighboring poem, "At the Fishhouses," and apply that knowledge to this place and situation. "Out on the high 'bird islands,' Ciboux and Hertford," readers enter a world removed from and yet sinisterly impregnated by human habitation. The relatively comical "razorback auks and the silly-looking puffins" stand as ceremonial guards along the cliff's edge "with their backs to the mainland." Humanity's presence, however, is everywhere: in the "pastured sheep," in the frightening airplanes that threaten them, in the "rapid but unurgent [pulse] of a motorboat." More than humanity's "unnatural presence" threatens the islands, which are surrounded and upheld by the heartless immensity of the Melvillean sea; as the ocean seems its calmest, it turns most hazardous. Effortlessly, Bishop draws attention from the placid uncertainties of the landscape to the more threatening uncertainties of the sea:

> The silken water is weaving and weaving,
> disappearing under the mist equally in all directions,
> lifted and penetrated now and then
> by one shag's dripping serpent-neck . . . .

> [CP, 67]

The times and tides of Bishop's sea form and enact their own fate. Bishop does not rely solely upon the sea to produce such mysterious effects. The fog blocks the various natural penetrations and rents in the earth's surface—"the valleys and gorges of the mainland"—further suggesting the difficulty of isolation peculiar to the islands. The poet introduces the spiritual, unearthly world to draw us toward but not into the formative, causative world beyond the poem. The essence of this otherworldly island world lies buried

> among those folds and folds of firs: spruce and hackmatack—
> dull, dead, deep peacock-colors,
> each riser distinguished from the next
> by an irregular nervous saw-tooth edge,
> alike, but certain as a stereoscopic view.

Bishop points to origins with the processional solemnity of "dull, dead, deep," but quickly returns to the constraints of the quotidian. Moore's "A Grave"—where "The firs stand in a procession, each with an emerald turkey-foot at the top"—and Stevens's "Domination of Black" echo throughout this stanza. The "striding" color of "heavy hemlocks" and the cry of the peacocks in the Stevens poem suggest a sudden onset of perception and fear. Bishop's descriptive language parallels Stevens's imaginative world of tropes in acknowledging the interface between reality and the unknown, this world and the next. Stevens's fear of the peacock's cry stems from his discomfort with his ignorance, while Bishop allays a comparable anxiety by sharing the uncertainties engendered by the irregularities that characterize the scene. At the midpoint of "Cape Breton" Bishop seems willing to risk (in Keatsian fashion) the terrible revelations that occur when one "look[s] too far into" a landscape.

The third stanza opens with a reckless, if comical, abandon that indicates a radical change of tone or a penetration of the poem's surface tension. Here lurks the first hint of the presence of humankind since the ghostly pulsations of the motorboat at the opening. Human works check the flow toward interiority. The island idles on this Sunday as its earthmovers stand driverless, but the mere presence of those objects tempers the movement toward epiphany. Not only has work ceased but so has religious activity:

> The little white churches have been dropped into the matted hills
> like lost quartz arrowheads.

The churches themselves are relics of another age and spiritual condition. The road is not a thoroughfare but rather the borderline between the experiential landscape and the interior, "where we cannot see." Within,

> where deep lakes are reputed to be,
> and disused trails and mountains of rock
> and miles of burnt forests standing in gray scratches
> like the admirable scriptures made on stones by stones —

lies the earth's own record. Bishop suggests, however, that by its very uninhabitable nature, the landscape defies translation. She suggests that the real story has passed; human life has occurred after the fact:

> and these regions now have little to say for themselves
> except in thousands of light song-sparrow songs floating upward
> freely, dispassionately, through the mist, and meshing
> in brown-wet, fine, torn fish-nets.

Bishop does not share Keats's view of the nightingale as "immortal Bird," but she is well aware of the poetic convention of birdsong as a tentative link between exterior and interior worlds. In "Cape Breton," though, the sparrow songs and the torn netting pull the poem in a direction Bishop does not wish to follow. The fishnet metaphor, derived from Penelope's weaving and the handi-

work of the Fates, engages the inarticulate, magical creative imagination. The introductory movement of "At the Fishhouses" acknowledges this ominous weight, and uses it to further explore the
relationship between netter and net, and by extension, poet and
poem. In "Cape Breton," however, the metaphorical insistence of
the nets seems beyond the intended scope of the poem. They and
the dangling notes of the song-sparrows drift into and become one
with the world beyond her poetry. This marks a turning point,
requiring either transcendence or a naturalistic embrace of these
natural hieroglyphics to honor, as Bishop always does, the legibility
of the text. Drawing attention from the celestial distractions, however, Bishop shifts the focus to the road below, which in following
an erratic but earthly course asserts the power of human culture,
especially its most mundane occasions, to place natural transcendence under erasure.

As a figure of narration, rather than of lyric ecstasy or brooding
meditation, this "wild" road serves as a measure of limits and ca-
pacities. The confines of the bus, "packed with people, even to
its step," frame the pilgrimage, "It passes . . . It stops," and the
availability of domestic knowledge:

> . . . a man carrying a baby gets off,
> climbs over a stile, and goes down through a small steep meadow,
> which establishes its poverty in a snowfall of daisies,
> to his invisible house beside the water.

The family life of the baby-carrying gentleman remains in the imagination; his house, literally out of sight, is unrealized. The poet
curiously regards the other guardians of the interior space; just
two more passengers, "but today only two preachers extra, one
carrying his frock coat on a hanger," no different really in capacity
from, say, the weekday "groceries, spare automobile parts, and
pump parts." Like the tiny churches littering the hillside, these men
of faith seem anachronistic.

"Cape Breton," like "The Monument," repeatedly shifts its
stance at the onset of epiphanic moments. Bishop is ostensibly
shifting her viewpoint, but for what purpose? What does she hope
to accomplish by moving from an island profile to a mist-shrouded
glimpse of the settled mainland, and then to the departures and
arrivals of a bus trip? In the final stanza, apparently on the brink

of epiphany, an odd reversal occurs. Linked to the final lines of "At the Fishhouses," the first line of the closure of "Cape Breton" — "The birds keep on singing, a calf bawls, the bus starts" — does not surprise. This assertive continuity is pure Bishop. Yes, the reader assents, this is true. Here, however, differing from more characteristic Bishop closures, an epiphanic suggestion of the otherworldly enters. The cloaking chill has its roots in *pre*history, beyond "earthly trust." How different the effect of the last stanza would be if Bishop had chosen to retain the final word, to deliberately limit her poem's world:

> The thin mist follows
> the white mutations of its dream;
> an ancient chill is rippling the dark brooks.
> The birds keep on singing, a calf bawls, the bus starts.

This remains for Bishop a rather open closure; the poem halts at a moment in which nature and culture seem in verbal congruence. The "ancient chill," reminiscent of the "chill white blast of sunshine" in "A Cold Spring," invokes the world of the unknown that engenders the brooks, calves, birds, and even buses of the phenomenal world.

When Bishop sorted and recast her memories of a bus trip from Nova Scotia to Boston, she made a poem of confrontation and exchange with nature that verges on epiphany, but retreats at the last moment into the natural domesticity of the creature world. "Back to Boston" (the working title for "The Moose" [G]) bears the lineaments of an actual bus trip, but turns into a response to romanticism and what she saw as its conflict with life. Situating the narrator in the trope of westward travel, she builds toward and then deviates from an expected epiphany; rather than fully develop her trope, she prefers to pause and reflect upon the "little of our earthly trust," confounding nature and culture in an embodiment, a creature that is neither threateningly wild nor sentimentally tame.

The measured sestets replicate the moral increments of the human condition. Unlike the repeated sameness of "At the Fishhouses" ("I have seen it over and over, the same sea, the same, / slightly, indifferently swinging above the stones") or the monotony of the landscape of "Crusoe in England" ("The sun set in the same sea, the same odd sun rose from the sea"), the habits of the natural world of "The Moose" are vaguely reassuring, predictable, repeatable. The Möbius strip — winding and returning — six-stanza, single-sentence introduction creates a recognizable, though not necessarily specific, landscape. The scene defies placement on a map, but its characteristics are predictable. The world depicted in this journey-poem sustains the speaker with glimpses of domesticity to counter the dark and the unease of travel. Inhabited by consumers of "fish and bread and tea," the landscape offers security in spite of the flux of travel and of the poem itself.

The herrings, the sun, and even the church depend on the will of the sea, which invests the land with life and uncertainty. The vulnerable landscape penetrates the very vehicle of discovery in the poem, the bus:

> through late afternoon
> a bus journeys west,
> the windshield flashing pink,
> pink glancing off of metal,
> brushing the dented flank
> of blue, beat-up enamel

[CP, 169]

The mortal substance of the bus reminds us of those "Under the Window" vehicles that so eloquently raised the issues of health and disease (the Mercedes-Benz truck with "Throbbing rosebuds" and the old truck with "a syphilitic nose"). Even as the bus displays a vaguely human anatomy, it reveals a relatively human temperament as it goes

> down hollows, up rises,
> and waits, patient, while
> a lone traveller gives
> kisses and embraces
> to seven relatives
> and a collie supervises.

The solitary traveler bids farewell to her kind, while the dog, a guardian of stationary domesticity, presides over the departure into the unknown. Linking the fixed and the mobile worlds in this genre scene gives the landscape an air of unity and harmony. By drawing the introduction together with a series of *where*s and *past*s, in the present tense, Bishop emphasizes the predictable, accountable, acceptable aspects of the scene.

As certainly as the traveler relinquishes family and home, the poem relinquishes the comfortable but momentary stasis of the genre scene, along with the scene itself. The true journey begins; the poem abandons the tropes of place-specific domesticity (elms, farm, dog) that embody family, home, and landscape. The mist, a painterly element, drifts in to shroud, enfold, and disclose the dislocating countenance of the natural surroundings. As the familiar world fades in the mist, the poem shifts its attention to a world of diminished scale and microscopic form:

> The bus starts. The light
> grows richer; the fog,
> shifting, salty, thin,
> comes closing in.
>
> Its cold, round crystals
> form and slide and settle
> in the white hens' feathers,
> in gray glazed cabbages,
> on the cabbage roses
> and lupins like apostles . . .

The atmosphere, though hardly threatening, rapidly grows murky. The "sweet peas cling" to their strings and the "bumblebees creep / inside the foxgloves" for certainty and shelter. As the fog obscures it adheres, transforming phenomena and affecting behavior. Whatever predictability this world possessed in daylight has receded in obscurity. Potentially magical as this landscape had become, it in no way resembles the celestial world of "Seascape" or the iridescent world of "At the Fishhouses." Bishop is determined to avoid tropes of sublimity (though toying with Wordsworth's Snowdon mist) and make this bus-trip only as rich as everyday life.

The gradual descent into evening (announced by "evening commences") occasions a renewed commitment to routine, which offsets the slide into the romantic otherworld of the fog. Frequent stops, signaling arrivals and departures, suggest the continued proximity of the familiar world. The routine of a household as "a woman shakes the tablecloth / after supper" adequately deters the Homeric sense of travel-as-epic. Evening domesticity, despite the passage of the vehicle, enacts its schedule, regular as the tides. Gradually, however, this artificial world yields to the unfocused (because sensory-deprived) world of disconnected sensations, a world unorchestrated by familiar motifs of order and routine:

> The Tantramar marshes
> and the smell of salt hay.
> An iron bridge trembles
> and a loose plank rattles
> but doesn't give way.

Destabilized by unexpectedly full sensory application, the poem drifts through a narrative of peripheral glances, partial appreciations. Even as the postprandial woman fades in that flickering instant, the bus slips into a cloaked land and sea world where the salt marsh sensationally reveals its true and frightening origins. Human structures quake in the uncertainty of this setting; they react in "fear" as they "tremble" and "rattle." Though they stand firmly, if dubiously, those structures (and the traveler) feel collapse may be imminent. Once again the poem prepares the reader to meet the otherworldly. Though reduced to noting particulars— synecdoches of books and bark—the traveler attempts to impose some structure on a formless environment, and in doing so risks epiphany:

> On the left, a red light
> swims through the dark:
> a ship's port lantern.
> Two rubber boots show,
> illuminated, solemn.
> A dog gives one bark.

This fixed, solemn scene is more than sufficient to trigger an epiphany and render the bus journey a romantic narrative into sublimity and otherworldliness; but the moment passes, ungrasped. The entrance of a particularized, characterized, destined human being interrupts the moment of epiphanic possibility. Her personal characteristics, as she enters "brisk, freckled, elderly" to encounter her fellow travelers, underscore her ordinary, reassuring earthiness, as if to assert in her bearing the sufficiency of this phenomenal world. With her words to the bus driver, "All the way to Boston," the pilgrimage gains definition and a final destination. Having finally mapped the excursion and avoided premature closure, the poem returns to the preparatory atmosphere that clarifies even as it clouds.

Misty night landscapes and travel constitute a familiar romantic motif. Primed with specific literary sensations, the poem generates a powerful but familiar conjunction between the "moonlight and mist." The landscape—"hairy, scratchy, splintery"—however, like the "brisk, freckled, elderly" traveler, resists the ascent into a symbolic mode. Eased by the consonantal texture of the material world, the speaker forsakes romance and allegory and reclines toward sleep. This moment of partial oblivion invokes the antecedent world of memory:

> Snores. Some long sighs.
> A dreamy divagation
> begins in the night,
> a gentle, auditory,
> slow hallucination . . . .

Sprung from but simultaneously divorced from the surrounding matrix of landscape and domesticity, the poem now drifts into the language of ancestry and archetype. Though relying on unsorted and scattered particulars, Bishop relates her speaker to humanity as a whole, and more firmly anchors her in the historical world of culture, by means of an overheard, extended flow of anecdote and genealogy, narrated by anonymous yet firmly characterized interlocutors:

> In the creakings and noises,
> an old conversation
> — not concerning us,
> but recognizable, somewhere,
> back in the bus:
> Grandparents' voices
>
> uninterruptedly
> talking, in Eternity:
> names being mentioned,
> things cleared up finally;
> what he said, what she said,
> who got pensioned;

> deaths, deaths and sicknesses;
> the year he remarried;
> the year (something) happened.
> She died in childbirth.
> That was the son lost
> when the schooner foundered.

Devoid of immediate personal significance, these recollections of strangers revolve upon the common organic insults of "deaths, deaths and sicknesses." These consequential events, though requiring narration, stand isolated against the flow of history. Death itself, an abstraction commemorated in black-bordered obituaries is random and commonplace, yet humanly fascinating. Death occupies the poet's attention in the way that births and marriages do, as dignifying aspects of the quotidian. Mention of the archaic tragedy—"the schooner foundered"—elevates the discussion even beyond the elevated quotidian to touch upon a mythic dimension and a classic sense of the tragic. Catastrophic events, however, derive their significance from their fatal outcome. The universality of this closure makes it more bearable, more conversational, less newsworthy. Bishop notes the lack of impact of old news in her survey of "The Bight" [CS]:

> Some of the little white boats are still piled up
> against each other, or lie on their sides, stove in,
> and not yet salvaged, if they ever will be, from the last bad storm,
> like torn-open, unanswered letters.
> The bight is littered with old correspondences.

> [CP, 60]

Finally the tide of specificity affects only the living; a dreamy retrospect leaves us meditating dates that resonate—"the year (something) happened"—long after the significance of the event has withered. Shuttling pronominal exchanges invite the auditor into this world of common history, prompting recall of those universal characters who went "to the bad." The tentacular frame of reference outlines a common family tree. Individuality, the raw particulars, dissolve in a repetitious history of insults, injury, and events. The drone of recurrence secures and assures the listener while imposing a sense of commonality through disaster.

The traveler in "The Moose," withdrawing from recognition and resignation—"Life's like that. / We know *it* (also death)."—cuddles down into a child's secure understanding and relaxed confidence. Life passes in tranquillity, grandparents droning

> in the old featherbed,
> peacefully, on and on,
> dim lamplight in the hall,
> down in the kitchen, the dog
> tucked in her shawl.
>
> Now, it's all right now
> even to fall asleep
> just as on all those nights.

Though at first this dream-world excursion seems to reach beyond the phenomenal world, Bishop withdraws, reorders, and projects the dream into the quotidian world of her poem. In spite of the childlike acceptance of everything predictable and routine, the language of the memory-passages is that of adult recall. An earlier version shows that Bishop had originally intended a childlike passage similar to the innocence of "Five Flights Up" [G]:

> Now, it is safe now
> to go asleep
> Day will take care of things.
>
> [Typescript Draft]

> The little dog next door barks in his sleep
> inquiringly, just once.
> Perhaps in his sleep, too, the bird inquires
> once or twice, quavering.
> Questions—if that is what they are—
> answered directly, simply,
> by day itself.
>
> [CP, 181]

As Robert Hass suggests, these midnight inquiries reassure by firmly situating the poem in the conscious world—"being and being seen."

The encounter with the moose coincides with and benignly disrupts a false and earthbound self-assurance. Rather than reaching for the epiphanic sublime, Bishop summons one reasonably modest (though impressive in its own right) particular of the natural world. In the context of expected epiphany, this creature seems reassuring, only modestly awe-inspiring. Like the Poundian periplum, the encounter is indeed a sighting, a looking on the horizon, but it is certainly not comparable to the grandeur and spiritual pretension of a Wordsworthian natural revelation, nor does it offer the psychological certainty of Joyce's urban epiphanies. The moose initiates the exchange and actually experiences the bus:

> It approaches; it sniffs at
> the bus's hot hood.

Lacking gender, the creature appears at first both otherworldly and threatening; it seems a force unto itself. The curious animal beckons the dreamy travelers to consciousness. Unlike the retreating farmhouses and churches of the traveler's landscape, the presence stands solid, comfortable, and inspirational:

> Towering, antlerless,
> high as a church,
> homely as a house
> (or, safe as houses).

"Towering," vaguely threatening, but "antlerless," somewhat tamed, the moose straddles the worlds of nature and culture, embodying a domestic sense of wholeness. Dwarfed by the unassuming grandeur of the natural world, the passengers resort to childish utterances of the commonplace and obvious, further emphasizing the creature's domestic appearance and demeanor:

> "Sure are big creatures."
> "It's awful plain."
> "Look! It's a she!"

Unembellished nature on a scale both intimate and impressive startles the passengers, but their commonplace expressions help ward off the sublime. A mute and mild moose, with its relative bulk, silence, curiosity, and sex, affects but does not intimidate them.

The moose does not in the least resemble the battered, defeated fish ("I looked into his eyes . . . / They shifted a little, but not to return my stare") or Crusoe's goats with their blank, malicious eyes. Instead, like the seal of "At the Fishhouses," the moose participates in a direct encounter and exchange. The moose "sniffs" and "looks the bus over," as if in recognition of this fellow creature, vehicle and passengers complimented by its interest in their otherness. The casual yet intimate relationship between moose and travelers demonstrates how "earthly trust" includes all surface-dwellers; as the animal senses the people, so the Boston-bound passengers experience the moose:

> For a moment longer,
>
> by craning backward,
> the moose can be seen
> on the moonlit macadam;
> then there's a dim
> smell of moose, an acrid
> smell of gasoline.

The essential fact grows dim and is finally displaced by the smell of gasoline, which complements the moose's own scent. Though posed for transcendence, the poem at the moment of confrontation retreats into domesticity and the commonplace, the marvelous transforming environment serving to sensitize and alert the travelers to the precious life they share without violating the poem's essential self-containment by evoking the sublime.

Though suspicious of the romantic hejira and the epiphany, Bishop employs their strategies while avoiding the moment of commitment to the ineffable of the infinite. The otherness of nature is but half a perception; nature sees human presence as unnatural and curious. Rather than strive to penetrate or transcend the phenomenal world, Bishop attempts to define domesticity in relation to otherness, to learn by deferring the language of the interior to more clearly experience the language of the palpable world of surface and texture. Finally she asks, "What does nature make of us?"—underscoring the unbridgeable difference between the self and the exterior world.

Bishop attempts to pose an accurate relationship with the environment. Human limitations—destinations, schedules, births, deaths—mirror environmental complexities. Like Darwin, she delights in the natural world because it is natural; she sees the moose not as an emissary from the beyond but as a moose—and marvels at its "mooseness." Generating a language of the environment without attempting to confound it with the self empowers the quotidian, with its hint of epiphanic possibility, which for Bishop is the proper material of poetry.

The act of naming, the other rhetorical device referred to at the beginning of this chapter, in romantic poetics begins with and requires the invocation of the social construct of authorship. Autobiography, a characteristic romantic-modern mode, enforces the notion of the voice of witness as one of authenticity and authority. This claim to authority, however, which was explored in Wordsworth's *Prelude* and claimed by modern poets like Robert Lowell, troubled Bishop. Her lifelong debate with herself concerning the tensions between life and authorship, autobiography and poetry surface repeatedly in her correspondence with Lowell. What she claimed of Marianne Moore (in her memoir, "Efforts of Affection"), she would claim of herself: "to be a poet was not the be-all, end-all of existence." In December 1957, when both poets were in the midst of their life studies, Bishop wrote to Lowell:

> And here I must confess . . . that I am green with envy of your kind of assurance. I feel that I could write in as much detail about my Uncle Artie, say — but what would be the significance? Nothing at all. . .
> Whereas all you have to do is put down the names! And the fact that it seems significant, illustrative, American, etc., gives you, I think the confidence you display about tackling any idea or theme, seriously, in both writing and conversation.

The seriousness of this lament is offset by Bishop's "green with envy" sly aside. Though she sees a collateral relationship between "significance" and "confidence," this does not confirm a sense of insecurity on her part. Rather, I suggest, she recognizes the need for a different kind of authorial posture for herself. If name-dropping and historical context will not work for her, what will?

Bishop requires a fresh approach to the question of authorial presence and its consequences for a poetry conscious of the problems of naming and unnaming. She intuits and anticipates the crisis of authorship and the literary text discussed by Michel Foucault in "What Is an Author?" Foucault suggests that modern literary critics continue to believe that:

[T]he author provides the basis for explaining not only the presence of certain events in a work, but their transformations, distortions, and diverse modifications (through his biography, the
determination of his individual perspective, the analysis of his
social position, and the revelation of his basic design).

Like Foucault, Bishop challenges the romantic assumption of authorial presence. Further, she asks her readers to socialize the
poem, to recognize its full range of significance, in the absence of
conventional authorial sanction. The confidence of these poems
derives from abandonment: the act of naming becomes one of
unnaming. Biography, social position (Bishop appears to be saying), as pre-existent constructs with authority outside of the text,
have no place in these poems.

"In the Waiting Room" and "Crusoe in England"—the opening
poems of *Geography III*—read intertextually reveal just how
deeply and ironically Bishop engaged in the relationship between
the self and author, history and memory, orality and literacy, naming and unnaming—indeed, in the binary oppositions of her aesthetic. It is this rhetoric of unnaming that generates the complexity
(not the debility) of self-reference and the provisional meaning not
only in her last works but throughout her career. Here the poems
beckon and then thwart the reader intent on finding significance
embedded in a life. The reader obsessed with the mock reality of
life will never encounter the real in Bishop's world.

"In the Waiting Room" and "Crusoe in England" enact competing genealogies of social and personal identity. Insofar as these
poems may be read as poems of poetic calling, they bear the testimony of a poet resolute in her determination to designate a fictional self without recourse to the power of naming conferred by
the social construct of authorship, and to force authority, instead,
from unnaming. This rejection of the self as social construct and
privileged naming may seem even more romantic than the solipsism
of authorship because it attempts to reinvigorate the originative
power of naming. Bishop, however, neither claims access to origins
nor refuses the social meaning imposed by language and culture.
Instead she attempts to displace the romantic concept of authorial
autonomy, because it is a received and therefore logocentric social
construct, and install through unnaming and renaming a more

broadly mediated sense of things and experience, a socially rather than egoistically based phenomenology.

"In the Waiting Room" may be seen as a prelapsarian poem of anticipation of that social state that precedes the acceptance of received namings; "Crusoe in England" may be read as a postlapsarian meditation on the originating power of naming and renaming. In reinventing the social world that connects the two, she seems willing to reconsider all forms of "name" appropriation: place, family, sex, generation, things. Discovering a world where (as Stevens found) "Mrs. Anderson's Swedish baby / Might well have been German or Spanish," she then rejects all such forms of naming as well as (what Foucault calls) "author construction." Each poem reenacts "birth, procreation, and death" as a debate between naming and unnaming, the loss imposed by a social (i.e., authorial) identity.

In 1961, Bishop wrote "The Country Mouse," a posthumously published memoir dedicated to her childhood return to Worcester, Massachusetts, after a lengthy stay with her maternal grandparents in Nova Scotia. Were it not for its startlingly revealing conclusion, the memoir, in spite of its abundance of details, would suffer from (by Bishop's own standards) insignificance. In the final paragraphs, however, which constitute the nucleus of "In the Waiting Room," Bishop begins to trouble over the obvious: the social obligation of being human. Having been jolted into awareness of her adoptive family's class status (*hers* was a family with servants), she recalls with equal sensitivity the *strangeness* of being a human being. As she waits for her aunt in the dentist's waiting room:

> I felt . . . *myself*. In a few days it would be my seventh birthday.
> I felt *I, I, I,* and looked at the three strangers in panic. I was *one*
> of them too, inside my scabby body and wheezing lungs. "You're
> in for it now," something said. How had I got tricked into such a
> false position? I would be like that woman opposite who smiled
> at me so falsely every once in a while.

> [CPr, 33]

The history of identity is bound to the memory of its occasion. The response is visceral, *not* intellectual:

> "You are you," something said. "How strange you are, inside
> looking out. You are not Beppo, or the chestnut tree, or Emma,

you are *you* and you are going to be *you* forever." It was like coasting downhill, this thought, only much worse, and it quickly smashed into a tree. *Why* was I a human being?

The fact of this prerational recognition scene resides in the primacy of childhood identity. The duplicity the child hears and sees in the adult world can only be named by those understudy pronouns: *I* and *you*. While dogs, trees, and even servants have names, this as yet unnamed child wrestles with but a taxonomic classification: human.

"In the Waiting Room" marks Bishop's return to these issues of naming and unnaming, reading and writing, sounding and hearing. Though descriptive, the poem depends less on physical detail and more upon a dialogue between the unnamed (socially unrestricted) self — "I" — and the named (socially restricted) — "an *I*." The child initially finds security in proper names: "Worcester, Massachusetts" and "Aunt Consuelo." The certainty fades with the appearance of the intrusive, indefinite pronoun: "*It* was winter. *It* got dark / early" [my emphasis]. Bishop will rely upon the ambiguity of "it" and its corresponding reluctance or inability to name throughout the poem.

Left alone, the child "I" sees and reads the named *National Geographic*. Its "studied photographs" reveal an unpredictable, eruptive (prelapsarian) landscape. Literacy fails, except as an escape route, where metaphor is concerned. Investigating scenes from this magazine, she catalogues that which she can name: volcano erupting, Osa and Martin Johnson. Properly attired people bear names: "Osa and Martin Johnson"; dead people lose their names: " — 'Long Pig,' the caption said." Orality and literacy compete for the child's attention, each seductive in its way. But she mis*hears* what "the caption sa[ys]": "A dead man slung on a pole / — "Long Pig." Mimicking the instability of spoken language and substituting a euphemism for a proper name, the conversational caption confuses the earnest student, who fails to understand that the dead man is here regarded as a food source.

The verbal unknown occasions further confusion as the child's eye traces the physical, sexual uncertainties of uncovered women. So foreign are the native unnamed women "with necks / wound round and round with wire" that the child "reads" right through them: "I read *it* straight right straight through. / I was too shy to stop" [emphasis added]. Unable to name, the child resorts to the tense comfort of the unnamed: "it." She retreats from the shifting planes of unnamed, unnamable uncertainty to the fixity of that which bears a name: "the cover: / the yellow margins, the date." Such is the force of Dickinson's notch in the maelstrom.

Unable to read her way into the larger constellation of human beings, the child nevertheless recognizes the sounded family identity when she hears it. Like the auditor in "The Country Mouse," this child hears from the inside out. History and memory fuse, creating a new identity for her:

> What took me
> completely by surprise
> was that it was *me*:
> my voice, in my mouth.
> Without thinking at all
> I was my foolish aunt,
> I — we — were falling, falling,
> our eyes glued to the cover
> of the *National Geographic*,
> February, 1918.

> [CP, 160]

The intensity of this "it" draws upon the accumulated chain of reference: "winter," "dark early," "Babies with pointed heads," "horrifying breasts," and Aunt Consuelo's "*oh!* of pain." Acceding to the social demands, the effect of her aunt's voice, the child involuntarily discovers her own collective voice: *I* becomes *we*. Dates, like names or Aunt Consuelo's voice, momentarily pierce the surface of the "cold, blue-black space" — the sea of habit threatening the child's consciousness. She has lost perceived autonomy even as she has gained a social identity.

Cautiously authorial, the child reads this new self as a mode of being. For the moment the discovery is personal, familial. This is not an attempt to place a "Bishop" in context; rather, it is an opportunity to feel a "self" move forward and backward into genealogy, into time:

> But I felt: you are an *I*,
> you are an *Elizabeth*,
> you are one of *them*.

Unlike the familial significance attributed to Lowell by Bishop, the effectiveness of Bishop's self-reading derives from the strategic use of the second person. As if to demonstrate her presence in the text, she removes her self from it long enough to proclaim a social identity, to name her self. This somewhat grudging sensation, verified spontaneously by the child's reaction to her aunt's cry, suggests the child's plight as it would seem from the outside. It recalls the Stevensian self: "Detect[ing] the sound of a voice that doubles its own." However "unlikely" or "strange" these binding "similarities" seem to the child they are the social facts of her life. Though they seem to her unauthorized, breasts, boots, the *National Geographic*, and the family voice nonetheless constitute homogenizing social realities. By adhering to the laws of pronominal reference, Bishop intensifies the almost Ibsenlike (recall the Button-molder of *Peer Gynt*) threat to an artist's emerging identity.

While "In the Waiting Room" has been routinely read as a poem of juvenile terror, isolation, and marginality, none of those readings account for the remarkable counterforce of the solitary "Me–Myself–I," the artist's isolated yet assertive self. Even if the unnamed self (as seen from the inside out) threatens to fail or consume, it remains the volatile poetry voice for Bishop. She may require (what Beckett calls) a "temporal specification"—"fifth / of February, 1918"—to allow her "to measure the days that separate [her] from that menace" (that which threatens identity). The "falling off" enacted in this poem is the fall into social identity, restrictive or inaccurate naming. The alternative seems to be the "big black wave" of annihilation or namelessness. To be "back in it" is to survive with a social surface—name, age, gender, place—at odds with the continually unnamed self. "The War was on" presages a career intensely committed to slipping the yoke of social identity and changing the rules of the name game.

The child of "In the Waiting Room" advances with uncertainty from the passivity of reader to the tentative aggressiveness of writer—to the authority of authorship. The socializing power of language itself lures the unnamed *I* into the realm of a given and feminine name—and perilously into the beyond of collective, pronominal identity: "one of them." This rush of potential identities refuses to pause at the brink of authorial privilege—*Elizabeth + Bishop*—and instead accelerates into the swirl of *them*. Refusing even gender specificity (recalling that in her memoir, Bishop ends with the more general "Why was I a human being?"), retaining no element of uniqueness, this identity is as good as none.

If the waiting room child must advance toward naming and its requisite social obligation, then "Crusoe at Home" (Bishop's working title for "Crusoe in England") has the life-won opportunity to revert to his unnamed *I*. Even as "In the Waiting Room" advances the cause of poetic naming, "Crusoe" champions the necessity of retreat. The child relinquishes ignorance for the sake of her name; Crusoe abandons the text and the very power of naming as if discovering the devitalizing force of individuation. Like other world-weary "I am" poems (John Clare's "I Am," Yeats's "The Circus Animals' Desertion," Wallace Stevens's "First Warmth" or "Notes Toward a Supreme Fiction"), "Crusoe" makes its most compelling appeal for readership by its utter rejection of its social role.

The landscape seems familiar; yet this volcanic wasteland is "dead as ash heaps." The colonial appropriators, or namers, are no longer in the characters of Osa and Martin Johnson; they have coalesced into the discovering and naming country itself: England. Decidedly postlapsarian, Crusoe both remembers and re-enacts that ahistorical, asocial moment of genuine love in exile.

Exasperated by the feminine, childhood aspects of the name game, Bishop turns from the dilemma of the given and family name to explore the old age of the retired adventurer. Crusoe, like Lowell, comes with his attendant significance — his fictive and historical authority. In spite of that burden, however, he shrugs off his social (i.e., linguistic) inheritance as irrelevant and inaccurate. Seemingly revisiting in memory the landscape of the *National Geographic* of "In the Waiting Room," Crusoe dismisses everything the child struggled to acquire. Orality and literacy fail to capture the essence of his life, which remains "un-rediscovered, un-renamable." The authorial gesture of the poem depends upon the exasperation that "None of the books has ever got it right." Like Ishmael, Crusoe knows that "true" places remain unnamed.

From Crusoe's perspective, to acknowledge the shock of "waiting room" recognition is to acquiesce to the failure of language to identify. The core of the poem, preceded by the weary "Well," charts the encumbrance of language in a solitary world. Relative scale ("I'd think that if they were the size / I thought volcanoes should be, then I had / become a giant"), proper names, aesthetics, categories of all kinds ring false in this underpopulated landscape of "one kind of everything." Here the distinctions between ignorance and understanding, error and truth seem impossible to ascertain. Who would appreciate the act of delimiting that naming reflects? The landscape seems fated to the same oblivion as language as Bishop echoes "The Map" (where "The names of the seashore towns run out to sea") in the volcanic landscape (where "The folds of lava, running out to sea, / would hiss").

Like the speaker in John Clare's "I Am," Crusoe, too, is a "self-consumer of [his] woes." Even in isolation this must be given a name and a circumstance: "'Pity should begin at home.' So the more / pity I felt, the more I felt at home." Crusoe resorts to this colloquy with himself to externalize and verify the overwhelmingly interior sensation of pity. The physical remove becomes palpable as he conjectures: "What's wrong *about* self-pity, anyway?" [my emphasis] Crusoe confesses his humanity through by naming his emotion. For as D. H. Lawrence asserts in his own "Self-Pity": "I never saw a wild thing / sorry for itself." Locating his emotion in language denies Crusoe the spontaneity or wildness of the animal world.

Incapable of "looking up" that which he does not possess, Crusoe abides by the asocial strictures of solitude. An air of unreality pervades the intense reality of this itemized landscape. Like the waiting-room child, Crusoe "reads" the landscape and attempts to place through names its inhabitants. His solitary word games seek to defeat "the questioning shrieks, the equivocal replies / over a ground of hissing rain": "*Mont d'Espoir* or *Mount Despair* / (I'd time enough to play with names)," but serve only to sound off: Names are rendered meaningless. Knowledge and language as social acts become nightmarish anachronisms:

> . . . . I'd have
> nightmares of other islands
> stretching away from mine . . .
> ....
> ....knowing that I had to live
> on each and every one, eventually,

> for ages, registering their flora,
> their fauna, their geography.
>
> [CP, 165]

Such occupational investments in local identity terrify the stranded character. As the waiting-room child discovered, even local geography requires an audience to render the significance fixed.

The eight-stanza terror of the societyless residence is peremptorily displaced by Crusoe's recollection of Friday. While language seems to have outlived its usefulness, Crusoe nonetheless fixes his "other" with a socially significant temporal marker: he names "Friday." Even as Crusoe details the effect of this new society, the impoverishment of language is complete. Declaring parenthetically that "Accounts of [Friday's arrival] have everything all wrong," he fails to meet the demands of language. Friday is "nice" and "pretty"; they were "friends." Stripped of a linguistic interface, Crusoe appears to have met the private, unmediated demands of a relationship shared with but one. Language cannot intervene.

The authorial impulse to give memory a name by converting it into history is a commemorative one. With Friday's deathdate comes the intrusive, factual marker—fixing in time the moment recalled, begging to be named. Crusoe's/Bishop's public and private artifacts seem destined for the Temple of the Muses: "The local museum's asked me to / leave everything to them." The human experiences of love and desperation coalesce about the devitalized remains: "the flute, the knife, the shrivelled shoes." Like Yeats's "Old iron, old bones, old rags," the island artifacts sit unre-discoverable and unrenameable. In questioning the value of this hopelessly romantic, Emersonian art of naming, Crusoe challenges the public appropriation of named things even as he re-collects the private bonding of language to love:

> How can anyone want such things?
> —And Friday, my dear Friday, died of measles
> seventeen years ago come March.

Unable to thwart the named order of things—names, dates, countries, diseases—Crusoe can only recall a time when the world was unnameable but "nice." Readers of Stevens will recognize both place and question: "These external regions, what do we fill them with / Except reflections, the escapades of death."

*

A reading of *Geography III* that considers the issues raised in discussing these two poems would presuppose a willingness to accept this paradox: that as autobiography abandons Bishop's poems, they begin to live. In American poetry only Dickinson has been as successful in frustrating critics who need to use the life as a means of explaining. Bishop's appreciation of Lowell's "kind of assurance" drove her to assert her confidence from the "interior," where, with due respect for the social and cultural energy that makes art possible, the poet is alone with the task of distinguishing her work from her self. Her life's sad facts do not explain why "we feel / (we all feel) this sweet / sensation of joy" when reading her poems and correspondence. Critics too eager to privilege autobiography over other forms of fiction to satisfy current critical trends risk reducing these multidimensional poems to self-elegy. This lack of critical imagination unduly restricts access to a body of work demanding recognition of its, not the poet's, authority.

The "old correspondences" littering *Geography III* can easily incite misreading, searching for poems definable by cultural or political communities Bishop herself rejected. Seeking the self Bishop deliberately withholds requires resisting a "knowledge . . . historical, flowing, and flown." This resistance denies the power of her assertive unnaming, forgetting that to be at war with something (in this case, restrictive identities) is in fact to confront it.

Extending this reading method to the entirety of *The Complete Poems, 1927–1979* reveals Bishop's career-long desire to subvert the "author-function," a desire largely fulfilled in the dialectic between autobiographical strategies and those of self-effacement. "Cape Breton" describes the resulting natural scene, which refuses the pathetic fallacy and turns a blank face to the viewer: "Whatever the landscape has of meaning appears to have been abandoned . . . these regions now have little to say for themselves." The private life inspiriting Bishop's poems cannot sustain them; they must live on their own, but they do so by first appropriating that private life and then placing it under erasure. The reader, faced with the transparent splendor of these poems, might wonder with the speaker of "Anaphora": "'Where is the music coming from, the energy? / The day was meant for what ineffable creature / we must have missed?'" As Foucault warns, "The author is the principle of thrift in the proliferation of meaning." Thriftier than most writers, and anxious that neither name nor gender restrict the authority of her poems, she withdraws, through unnaming, the authorial privilege by purposing, then exposing the feigned naïveté of autobiography. The resultant fiction in its complex reflexivity is too self-possessed for the reader or critic to unmask, and paradoxically refuses either to confound life and art or to clearly distinguish them.

CHAPTER 3

The Absent Mother

Like the child-persona Elizabeth of "In the Waiting Room," Bishop experiences and tests the world about her in search of a language sufficient to her experience, a language that would center her voice in relation to family, humanity, nature, and landscape. The interlocking tropes of self and the narrative frame of "In the Waiting Room," for instance, are merely more elaborate forms of the direction (or "pointing," as William James would say) of her work as a whole. In this and her other poems that elaborately situate a persona, the need is to generate texture sufficient to encourage a full empathy with the experiences they purport to embody. A poem like "In the Waiting Room" derives much of its power from its stance as a quiet moment along a journey, deriving much of its force from the larger trope. The journey-trope is doubled here, as in so many other poems, because not only is Worcester, Massachusetts, a physical place literally along the way, but it is also a stage in the pilgrimage out of childhood into experience. Thus, although the language privileges the exterior over the interior world (the child emphasizes herself, even perhaps against her will, as a social being), the poem preserves the doubleness of worlds through the double nature of the hidden but controlling trope of the journey.

This journey-trope is hardly original with Bishop, but it is one of the most persistent in literature. The Puritans struggled to center themselves in the (for them) competing worlds of nature and spirit through mastery of the resources of their language. Their plain style provides a model for effectively construing mutual tropes of socialization, individuation, and communication. When Emerson countered his own skepticism in "Experience" with "To know a little, would be worth the expense of this world," he expected us to recall the critical focusing demanded earlier. The reconstruction of selfhood through the "rounding" effect of the mind's eye, the refinement of selection through rhetoric, narration, and tone, together constitute a discernible form of knowledge of the world. This knowledge, in turn, generates and arranges a series of tropes, and the resultant poem displays a fictional but convincing model of this recreated world.

By centering her writing on experiential knowledge, Bishop enables herself to sound a vox humana, to limit herself to those occurrences capable of trying her readers. This is not to suggest that Bishop fails to acknowledge the affairs of the human heart; she merely relegates them to the interior, where language tends to founder with inadequate abstractions. Like Thoreau, Bishop knows that, "Experience is in the fingers and head. The heart is inexperienced." Her central trope of the traveler generates narratives of intellectual and sensual, rather than strictly emotional, growth. To discover a language adequate to embody the components and circumference of her world, she travels a course as rigorous and uncertain as Emily Dickinson's:

> I stepped from Plank to Plank
> A slow and cautious way
> The stars about my Head I felt
> About my Feet the Sea.
>
> I knew not but the next
> Would be my final inch —
> This gave me that precarious Gait
> Some call Experience.

Dickinson inches along the metaphors that characterize her life, discovering that despite her mooring in the physical world—the "slow and cautious way" of planks—she remains surrounded by the fluid and frightening unknown, the depiction of which requires a leap into abstract language. The awareness of mortality throughout, the element of peril, gives this linear creep—"Experience"—a particularly hazardous dimension. Dickinson sees making tropes of mortality the supporting planks of experiential knowledge. Without rhetorical awareness of the journey, such travels would be pointless because they would lack individuation through language. Dickinson and Bishop both find that the journey, a crucial trope of coming-into-being, is the best strategy to sustain their self-invention.

In spite of her wide use of tropes of knowing, including the journey, Bishop only once defines the "knowledge" of her poems. The final movement of "At the Fishhouses" [CS] risks using the sea, a powerful and ambitious metaphor that postulates knowing as a fluid, expressive, but chaotic, absorptive, and formless process expressed by the modifiers of "knowledge," "dark, salt, clear, moving, utterly free." The line that introduces this closing metaphor asserts that the relationship between knowledge and imagination is definitive: "It is like what we imagine knowledge to be." Changed in the third typescript from "This is what I imagine knowledge to be," this line asserts the social, rather than the individual, import of this metaphor. Seasoned by a sensory immersion, the rhetorical flow must now abstract that sensational knowledge into the matrix of a historical yet nondogmatic understanding. Despite the firm antecedent link to the sea, this *it* shimmers with ambiguity. The poem struggles to remind itself that its ebb and flow of modifiers is securely moored in the sea, the figural, rhetorical function of which is as solid as its literal referent is fluid. The experience generated by the poem is primarily one of metaphor-awareness as a means of warding off or controlling the abstraction toward which all knowledge tends. Beyond metaphor lies metaphysics, in which, as Melville pointed out, it is easy to drown.

The personification of the shore world, immediately following the modifiers of "knowledge"—"the cold hard mouth / of the world, derived from the rocky breasts"—refuses accessibility to conventionally comforting ideas of motherhood in favor of raw origin. The security of the bedrock shore is the viewpoint it offers on origination and the concomitant peace of death, a physical vantage-point and a figurative irony. The sea, too, occupies both a figurative role (as knowledge, chaos, psychic depth, amniotic fluid) and a physically verifiable biological function as originary medium.

To expect wisdom or nourishment from the known but imaginatively dead shore-world is an error, but to step from it into the dark, salt, flowing sea is to be a transcendentalist, and suicidal. Not even the language of transcendence, then, can generate a fiction adequate to both the senses (the physical self) and the psyche (which finds its analogue in the sea). Knowledge, that troubling abstraction, leads beyond metaphor, beyond the apprehensible world. The poet cannot follow, but remains on the rocky, unnourishing shore, and gazes at the abstract, unobtainable freedom beyond, and infers, if she dares, the mysteries beyond the range of the senses. Yet it is precisely the act of discovering this limitation that is "historical," accretive, "flowing," organic, and "flown," perishing.

In "At the Fishhouses" Bishop speculates upon the province and parameters of the available language of knowledge and, by extension, the limitations of the role of metaphor and other kinds of figuration in her writing. Unlike the childlike question-and-answer scenario of "Five Flights Up," this meditation defines knowledge (or rather, defines the nature of knowledge) without restricting the source of inspiration. That is, in its act of linguistic and dramatic self-discovery, "At the Fishhouses" privileges the power of meditation and the assertive gaze of the speaker, rather than a particularly configured scenario limited or empowered by the stance, age, or available vocabulary of the speaker. Though Bishop's measured tone and insistence on the social dimension of knowledge bear little resemblance to Emerson's "perfect exhilaration" (an exhilaration that might have thrust Bishop's persona into the cold sea), the return to "reason and faith" resounds throughout the poem. Like those of Emerson's "lover of nature," Bishop's "inward and outward senses" remain "adjusted to each other" — she refuses to abandon herself to the enticing fluid vagueness that would extinguish those senses. Her orchestrating personality directs and empowers this scene, and retains control despite the undeniable implications of her meditation. As Emerson would explain this process of discovery in *Nature*:

> Yet it is certain that the power to produce this delight, does not reside in nature, but in man, or in a harmony of both . . . Nature always wears the colors of the spirit.

The poet of this marginal "Fishhouse" world (and its later companion piece, "The End of March" [G]) engages nature with a full awareness of the problematic relationship between language and the environment. Like Lowell's inchworm, Bishop is always "feeling for something to reach something"; her movement toward knowledge is an associative process. Grounded by her commitment to the figurative language of the senses, she reaches beyond her grasp, but faces the full implications of doing so.

Describing the wide variety of Bishop's tropes of knowing requires consideration not only of those poems of unhampered meditation, but those narrated by or concerning experience-poor travelers, children, and provincials as well. Like Keats in his Odes suppressing first one sense, then another, Bishop refines the trope of the journey by subjecting it to carefully delineated boundaries or frontiers. The initial dailiness of the child's world fails to provide interpretive skills comparable to those of the speaker of "At the Fishhouses" or "The Monument." The years of childhood, as Wordsworth demonstrates in the Immortality Ode, reflect in mimicry the motion of adult life. Bishop's provincial world offers an alternate view of innocence, not as a dangerous flaw (as Melville presents it in *Billy Budd*), but as a childlike realm impenetrable by her adult consciousness. These poems and stories of class and locale-deprivation share the aesthetic concerns but not the intellectual commitment of Bishop's childhood poems. While the childhood world is bombarded by particulars as apparently disparate as those of the provincial world, the expectation is one of synthesis, of organization into a whole, a reflective position aware of the past and future. The homely folk revel in particulars, the quotidian that is life stripped bare of its referential frame.

Unsurprisingly, the *autre fois* figures of child and provincial inform and speak to the larger issue of the family. As illustrated in the narratives of Grimm and Andersen, fairy tales exploit the aura of simplicity and unadulterated humanity embodied in depictions of children and rustics (the miller, the cobbler, the farmer). This world enclosed between "once upon a time" and "happily ever after" values familiar and predictable qualities, and postulates a quasi-historical concern with name, sex, social standing, talent, and comeliness. The singlemindedness of the child faced with the adult world supports no internal wisdom; the available language is

barely adequate to sketch the beginnings of self-knowledge and a
grasp of the world, concentrating, primarily, on the act of naming.

Childhood, viewed for much of human history merely as a pause
between infancy and adulthood rather than a well-defined state
of being, assumed no importance as a source and key to mature
consciousness until the nineteenth century. Only then did the West-
ern world engage in what Phillipe Ariès calls "the discovery of
childhood." As he explains in *Centuries of Childhood* (1962), "No-
body thought, as we ordinarily think today, that every child already
contained a man's personality. Too many of them died." Of the
nineteenth-century writers, Wordsworth and Dickens most successfully tapped those searing impressions for which psychology had
not yet invented a scientific language. The vitality of these threshold years inflames the Emerson of *Nature* and "Experience." In
Nature he finds that while the "sun illuminates only the eye of the
man . . . [it] shines into the eye and heart of the child." Respecting
every implication of the journey-trope at the center of the romance
of the individual life, he recognizes, too, the usefulness of mapping
the point of departure when the child first realizes the necessity of
moving on:

> The child asks, "Mamma, why don't I like the story as well as
> when you told it me yesterday?" Alas, child, it is even so with the
> oldest cherubim of knowledge. But will it answer thy question
> to say, Because thou wert born to a whole, and this story is a
> particular?

What captures the imagination of author and analyst alike is not
so much what is known (for that succumbs to petty eccentricities
and personalities), but how knowledge accumulates. How then can
either science or poetry account for the creation of an individual?
Bishop's attempt to discover or invent an adequate language of
self-knowledge properly begins with the record of childhood in the
Nova Scotia writings.

> The boat a very quaint sternwheeler made in the USA *70* years
> ago—everyone nice and polite, but each and every one asked if I
> had a "family" and when I said no, they all commiserated with
> me, but also, I felt, rather avoided me as being not quite all
> there.
>
> (Postcard to Ashley Brown, 1967)

The early death of her father, and the insanity and institutional-
izing of her mother, prompted Bishop to explore, even to exploit,
this sense of "being not quite all there." She achieves this exploration by possessing (what M. H. Abrams sees in Wordsworth and
Proust) "a double awareness of things as they are and as they
were." The language-awareness and available vocabulary of an
adult informs and directs the return to childhood, the place where
Bishop mythologizes as social reintegration what is in fact her self-
creation. The swirl of needs and stimuli, the carnival of the senses
adults associate with childhood, require Bishop to contrive metaphors of both understanding and learning (*connaître* and *savoir*).
Creating a convincing narrative of childhood and social development, for Bishop, is the measure of her success in reintegrating
herself into a society in which, in fact, she never assumed a full
role. This narrative requires a powerful series of meditative tropes,
inappropriate to the voice of a child but empowered by adult mis-
recollection. The psychic necessity of this endeavor empowers the
child-persona with language and purpose beyond her years but, in
this reconstruction, not at all beyond her needs.

The body of tropes, points of view, and tonal constructions in
these stories and poems fall into two broad categories: those of
received knowledge and those of acquired knowledge. In Bishop's
fictional reconstruction, the qualities of humanity derive not only
from genetic and genealogical inheritances (sex, race, family), they
also devolve from the masks and manners of common rituals (bap-
tisms, weddings, funerals). The child pantomimes adult roles until
in maturity she assumes her place. Yet coincidentally, the child
demands direction for herself, assuming the role of self-prophet, a
role only the adult perspective can grant her. The child repeatedly
experiences moments of self-discovery empowered by the selective
memory of the adult, who imposes history on the fictional present.
The child senses the elements, shapes, colors, textures, and begins
to synthesize through fictionally tentative understandings and misunderstandings of language.

Bishop initially scans her formative years in prose. *The New
Yorker* stories, "Gwendolyn" and "In the Village" (1953), predate
Robert Lowell's *Life Studies* by several years, suggesting a reciprocity between the two "autobiographies." "Gwendolyn," the more
conversational and obviously autobiographical of the two, exploits

the contrast of the interior tale of Gwendolyn with the frame of factual narration. In doing so, Bishop reveals the child's period of self-recognition and sexual self-discovery.

The two-part structure of "Gwendolyn"—that of the teller and the tale—explores the child's growing self-awareness and how that contributes to her posture of interpretation. The story addresses the problem of narrator reliability by delineating the child's view of her world so that the reader understands how to trust or mistrust her history of Gwendolyn. The child occupies a motherless realm, overseen by a grandmother and now absentee aunt, "away in 'the states' in Boston, training to be a nurse." Unlike many of Bishop's tales, this story requires that the child-narrator be a girl; the discoveries depend on it. Yet the narrator struggles uncomfortably with that necessity, seeming to claim that as a reflection of her "invalid" (pun?) state ("I had been sick with bronchitis for a long time."). The clash of health and illness is revealed in the child's dolls. Playing now with Aunt Mary's "Best doll . . . a girl doll," the child sees this as an ideal "companion to an invalid." Despite the intriguing vastness of the prized doll's wardrobe, it had suffered the ravages of months of use and moths and decay. The doll, itself, upon detailed inspection, is found to have lost a certain vitality and importance:

> She had lain in her drawer so long that the elastic in her joints had become weakened; when you held her up, her head fell gently to one side, and her outstretched hand would rest on yours for a moment and then slip wearily off.

> [CPr, 214]

This doll seems too fragile for the real world, lacking in substance beyond her wardrobe from "long drawers trimmed with tiny lace" to the splendor of the skating costume. The fanciful fragility of this doll demands a reassessment of the child's real companions:

> She made the family of dolls I usually played with seem rugged and childish: the Campbell Kid doll, with a childlike scar on her forehead where she had fallen against the fender; the two crudely felt-dressed Indians, Hiawatha and Nokomis; and the stocky "baby doll," always holding out his arms to be picked up.

The invalid has been forced to forsake these tough veterans of her health; these dolls were known more for their characters than their sexual identities (although it is interesting that the usually gender-less "baby doll" is a boy). Clearly this child feels shorn of her identity; she feels much of her is known by the company she keeps. Aunt Mary's deteriorating doll — all surface without substance — and the debilitating bronchitis season the child for the arrival of Gwendolyn.

Gwendolyn becomes a mirror of self-definition for the child, the reverse "other" figure in her life, insofar as she embodies the foreign fascination of Aunt Mary's doll. Gwendolyn Appletree seems lifted from the happy forest family of a fairy tale; her domestic world presents a comforting, relational structure previously unexperienced by the child-narrator. In further contrast, Gwendolyn's life suggests the possible range of childhood as a body of experience, and presents a well-developed genealogy as well:

> Gwendolyn Appletree was the youngest child and only daughter of a large, widely spaced family that lived away out, four or five miles, on a lonely farm among the fir trees. She was a year or so older than I — that is, about eight — and her five or six brothers, I suppose in their teens, seemed like grown men to me.

Unvoiced, a knowledge of self and sexuality emerges in the child, who sees in Gwendolyn the promise of another world — an unpromising one of responsibility and conventional femininity — as unlike her own as was Aunt Mary's doll. Gwendolyn embodies for the child "everything that the slightly repellent but fascinating words 'little girl' should mean." This rational child of seven has already distinguished herself from the others — the "little girls" — by contrasting Aunt Mary's doll with her own, which allows her to passively observe the like and the unlike, the I and Not-I. The child's experience with Gwendolyn takes its form from this comparison of dolls. Gwendolyn, in her fatal and fascinating diabetic sweetness, bears the feminine counterqualities so unwelcomed by the observant child. The overly fussy attentiveness of parents forever fearful of loss disgusts the tougher child and her grandmother, but the child understands that she must now confront, not merely observe, the distinctions noted between the dolls and apply them to her budding social awareness of Gwendolyn as a distinct Not-I with whom she must play.

An afternoon's tea party substitutes for the child's planned activities ("jump[ing] in the barn and swimming in the river") and provides a backdrop for an evening's education. The child's prized game (trapping bees in foxgloves) is also called off by the grandmother because of Gwendolyn's fragility. The afternoon concludes with an unexpected initiation:

> Our play was not without a touch of rustic corruption, either. I can't remember what happened, if anything, but I do remember being ordered out of the whitewashed privy in the barn after we had locked ourselves in and climbed on the seats and hung out the little window, with its beautiful view of the elm-studded "interval" in back of us.

The Freudian infantile amnesia of this privy scene (of prepositional succession) primes us for the discovery of self yet to come. The conventional, socially responsible conclusion, given the grandmother's harsh reprimand, is that the child's actions are *bad* (in a social sense) — and Gwendolyn is her victim. To learn, the child must confront the outer and inner forces of change. She needs a more sufficient language of exteriority and otherness, one that would enable her to consider Gwendolyn and girlhood and her "otherness" as dispassionately and clinically as Aunt Mary's doll.

An overnight stay, complete with shared bed, excites the child to the brink of knowledge — an awareness as threatening as it is intriguing. "Overwrought with the novelty," the child pursues her quest:

> I couldn't seem to make myself get into my side of the bed, so I went around and picked up Gwendolyn's clothes. She had thrown them on the floor. I put them over the back of a chair — the blue-and-white-striped dress, the waist, the long brown stockings. Her drawers had lace around the legs, but they were very dirty. This fact shocked me so deeply that I recovered my voice . . .

The recovery of her voice coincides with the discovery of her selfhood, or at least the absence of its denial. By seeing the shed, soiled femininity of Gwendolyn, the child finds worth in her own being. Gwendolyn has served her natural function, so is allowed to die — but not without one final threat to the security of the child's self-identity. The scene recalls that which Faulkner insisted was at the heart of *The Sound and the Fury*:

> "All right." Versh said. "You the one going to get whipped. I aint." He went and pushed Caddy up into the tree to the first limb. We watched the muddy bottom of her drawers. Then we couldn't see her. We could hear the tree thrashing.

Forever linking the somewhat "dirty" with the teasingly erotic, such scenes offer an opportunity to externalize as they represent the shifting, emerging sexual worlds of childhood and adolescence.

Barred from attending Gwendolyn's funeral, the child witnesses the passing in another way. As it did in the escape to the privy, the child's memory falters here; she recalls only the significance, not the occurrence (a combination of seen and imagined). Gazing through the lace-curtained window, the child sees Gwendolyn's coffin carried to, and then propped against the church. Unable to banish the spectacle of the little girl without a final peek, she stares:

> [S]traight through [the] lace curtain at Gwendolyn's coffin, with Gwendolyn shut invisibly inside it forever, there, completely alone on the grass by the church door.

The child knows the significance of that vision — "the exact sensation of that moment"; she was "familiar with it and recognized it" and had "already experienced it." She yokes it to an earlier tactile quest for a lost treasure, a remembered unexplainably forgotten present. The child has not only experienced Gwendolyn sensuously, but in the process has reflexively discovered her *self*.

Once again Aunt Mary's doll takes center stage, this time to explain death, not life. The child and clambering buddy, Cousin Billy, need to explain their discussions about "death in general." Demonstrations are required. In this process (the adorning of the nameless, stripped doll with flowers), the knowledge and experience fuse:

> She looked perfectly beautiful . . . I don't know which one of us said it first, but one of us did, with wild joy — that it was Gwendolyn's funeral, and that the doll's real name, all this time, was Gwendolyn.

The grandparental aftermath of fury is cloaked with forgetfulness; the child can only say, "I don't remember now what awful thing happened to me." By explaining Aunt Mary's doll, living through Gwendolyn, and rejoining the initial prop with Gwendolyn, the child has challenged the contrived surface of "little girlhood" and has come to know her true self through confrontation with her opposite. Throughout the tale, the various dolls represent a range of social projections unacceptable to the emerging artist. The child awakens to the problematic nature of such representations, sensing that the doll is not an adequate metaphor for her relationship to Gwendolyn. This sparks a premature insight into the problematic nature of art and its dubious relationship to actual issues of identity, sexuality, and becoming. The child, like the artist, must find her own "real name."

Studied sexuality dominates only one other childhood piece, the previously discussed "In the Waiting Room." This final debate about kinship, gender, and identity suggests that a child's identity is formed less by the accidents of birth (parentage, sex, family name) than by the individual's confrontation with and discovery of such "accidents." Until the child in "Gwendolyn" is forced to discover her differences (through the staged encounters with the doll and "little girl"), she exists in a self-assured, self-contained identity. The child sans context cannot know shame. This newly discovered context expands to a cultural one for the child "In the Waiting Room." The world of reading, studying, and exploring turns on the child and threatens her with potential identities and associations. Though she fails to explicitly bond to gender, the conjunction of *National Geographic* and "awful hanging breasts" suggest a relationship less to the community of human beings, and more to the "foolish and afflicted," like Aunt Consuelo.

Though nonpolemical in tone, these writings of self-discovery suggest a feminist dilemma for the child and the poet. In the absence of suitable role models (consider the images of women here), the child (girl) — quite unlike the "little girl" Gwendolyn or the "foolish, timid" Aunt Consuelo — is forced into rejecting a vital part of her being. How can this child find a place amid fools, skirts, and breasts? This issue requires discussion of the relational and phenomenal complexity of Bishop's childhood world, an exploration of her family. Only understanding how the child develops her own voice amid the family's "skein of voices" can account for her claim upon a language of selfhood.

In her *Paris Review* interview Bishop was candid about the difficulty of her family situation:

> My father died, my mother went crazy when I was four or five years old. My relatives, I think they all felt so sorry for this child that they tried to do their very best. And I think they did . . . But my relationship with my relatives — I was always sort of a guest, and I think I've always felt like that.

The failure of her family to provide a suitable role model is complete, and the attempts to console the child only succeed in emphasizing her forlorn status. At an age most receptive and most vulnerable, this child must look elsewhere for confirmation of self. Not only do rumors of impending dislocation persist in her family circle — a constant flux of residences and caretakers — but that actual and potential dislocation is both cause and metaphor of the child's inability to formulate a notion of self based on a strong sense of place and person. Despite the embarrassments imagined and recalled in Lowell's "91 Revere Street," for example, he never lacked the security of a fixed residence and a stable family unit.

Bishop creates a fictional persona raised by unduly fretful or careless ancestral figures. Overcautious of this to-be-pitied child, the circling relatives (an ominous weight on *that* word) seem to feel that they've been saddled with a depressing duty. The oppressive role of this constellation of caretakers indicates why the discovery of *girl*hood threatens this child. Despite or perhaps because of her relative precociousness, she is ill-prepared for confrontation with an interior self, which requires a history and a future, since she lacks any desirable or attainable model of adulthood.

These narratives of childhood are devoid of an acceptable or recognizable family. The father is altogether absent (or only appearing as the skeletal "man with buttons like tears" occupying the "rigid house" of the child's drawing in "Sestina"); the mother occurs only as a shrill perversion of the nurturer. Examination of the mother figure reveals why the child looks elsewhere for the mirror of her future self. Bishop employs conventional preconceptions of motherhood to emphasize the discord of her mother's presence. In so doing she provides the unexpected core of the child's awareness and perceptions.

Though she is rarely present in Bishop's writing, the mother-figure dominates, with her shadowy presence and more palpable absence, Bishop's entire body of writings about childhood. Her first depiction of the mother figure occurs not in a story or poem, but in her 1952 *Poetry* magazine review of Wallace Fowlie's *Pantomime*. Chiding Fowlie for his superficial and fanciful "autobiographical pieces," Bishop recalls her own Boston childhood:

> Tremont Temple and its Baptist sermons, Symphony Hall, the Harvard Glee Club, the Museum of Fine Arts — all these were part of my own childhood background, and as I read his book I could not help making comparisons between Mr. Fowlie's early impressions and my own. My own first ride on a swan boat occurred at the age of three and is chiefly memorable for the fact that one of the live swans paddling around us bit my mother's finger when she offered it a peanut. I remember the hole in the black kid glove and a drop of blood. I do not want to set myself up as a model of facing the sterner realities of swan boat rides in order to discredit Mr. Fowlie's idealization, — but there is remarkably little of blood, sweat, or tears in Mr. Fowlie's book.

Surely what gives the edge to these childhood stories and poems is Bishop's willingness to recall and face those "sterner realities." Yet that retrospective courage fails to prepare the fictional child for the kindlier present-tense aspects of self-discovery and childhood development. The omnipresent phantom of Bishop's youth — her mother — explains why the child's first discoveries of languages of self and otherness in "Gwendolyn" and "In the Waiting Room" prove both historical, in that they represent the missing mother, and prophetic in that they begin, however tentatively, to construct an internally generated model for the adult-to-be.

Like the Dickinson of "Nature — the Gentlest Mother is," conventional ideas of motherhood expect maternal presence to offer "Admonition Mild," "infinite Affection — / And infiniter Care." The motherly inheritance in this world, however, is one of discord that rends the child's consciousness even as it binds mother and child together. Bishop returns to meet both past and present in her 1965 collection, *Questions of Travel*, a two-part collection of poems

("Brazil" and "Elsewhere") hinged upon her "autobiographical fragment," "In the Village." Here the child is not merely threatened by indifferent adult figures and forms, she is also pierced by the insane presence of her mother. The child's nominally nurturing caretaker assumes the unpredictable form of a vulnerable demon. The negative and unsettled presence contaminates the village that had once given the child asylum (from her mother). The other's invasive presence fractures the most intimate bond in life (that umbilical bond of life and death), forcing mother and daughter into the suspended state of "she" and the child "I." As the mother's psychic state assumes the pitch of "a scream, the echo of a scream," it strains the psychological threads that tether the present-tense to the frightening, displaced, historical childhood years.

As Gaston Bachelard explains in *The Poetics of Space*, the home is a place where a child learns the "function of inhabiting"; it is the "first universe," to which he appends a qualified, restrictive definition: "All inhabited space bears the essence or the notion of home." Viewed in this light, Bishop's expatriotism and claim to perpetual guesthood expose the lack of the central shaping presence of a mother. The absence of the mother of "In the Village" is a palpable force. Narrative clues and familial imagery that suggests displacement, unease, confinement, and alienation suggest why the child-speaker's home is now in the house of her mother's mother:

> Before my older aunt had brought her back, I had watched my grandmother and younger aunt unpacking her clothes, her "things." In trunks and barrels and boxes they had finally come, from Boston, where she and I had once lived. So many things in the village came from Boston, and even I had once come from there. But I remembered only being here, with my grandmother.
>
> [CPr, 254]

Deprived of the maternal bond, the child finds the mother as a migratory, unstable, disruptive force. The family heart beats irregularly:

> First, she had come home, with her child. Then she had gone away again, alone, and left the child. Then she had come home. Then she had gone away again, with her sister; and now she was home again.

But not in the home of her own making: rather in the home of her birth.

As the child comes to see this grandmaternal home as her own, it affects the way she responds to her environment. The child has lost generational continuity, and with it a part of her identity. Because of this loss of selfhood she is unable to bond properly with her grandmother, who is too old, fussy, and uneasy anyway. As a shaping force, this home, perhaps because its tropes are solely those of age, resignation, and duty, molds a child in some ways more mature than usual, at least in this fictional recounting (the narrator of these stories is blessed with an irony, humor, and insight far beyond her years). The sad ancestral voices, however, cannot effectively guide the child into the present. Instead of serving as the child's fixed star, the mother becomes the prime variable in the child's life.

The emotional disturbance (manifested in the scream) disrupts not merely the relation between the mother and child, but also the sympathies of the satellite relatives. The very uniqueness of this uncertain childhood affects the learning process itself. The child is always trying to free herself from disrupting influences. The caretakers, those "responsible" relatives, feel compelled to care for the poor unfortunate child. However well-intentioned, they become oppressive forces to the child. A conventionally domestic kitchen scene reveals the disorientation of the home:

> My two aunts come into the kitchen. She is with them, wearing the white cotton dress with black polka dots and the flat black velvet bow at the neck. She comes and feeds me the rest of the porridge herself, smiling at me.
>
> "Stand up now and let's see how tall you are," she tells me.
>
> "Almost to your elbow," they say. "See how much she's grown."
>
> "Almost."
>
> "It's her hair."
>
> Hands are on my head, pushing me down; I slide out from under them.

As in the instance of the child awaiting Aunt Consuelo, this child's person is threatened by the terrifying outside world. Her caretakers do not mean to frighten, but their motives are faulty, and the fusion of love and guilt, conflated in their tentative and inadequate languages, muddles the home situation. A vocabulary of duty and obligation informs Bishop's childhood world. The grandmother's tendency to tears, the aunts' overly solicitous comforting of the child make this a fearfully protective environment: fearful not only because it is unsettled but because of the shadowy presence of her mother's inarticulate and unarticulated madness.

Like the boarding-house servant in Robert Frost's "A Servant to Servants" — "I have my fancies: it runs in the family. / My father's brother wasn't right" — the mother carries with her the fear of inherited insanity. So when she is finally committed to an asylum, the child knows not merely fear abated, but shame. The grandmother dispatches weekly packages to the institution, food for body and soul, and the child bears the responsibility of conveyance to the post office. She knows the stigma of mental illness and perceives it to be inescapable:

> The address of the sanitorium is in my grandmother's handwriting, in purple indelible pencil, on smoothed-out wrapping paper. It will never come off.

Even the child's best friend, Nate the blacksmith, must be shielded from this reality. Thus,

> Every Monday afternoon I go past the blacksmith's shop with the package under my arm, hiding the address of the sanitorium with my arm and my other hand.

The child denies a part of her self by this action; she literally denies her heritage. As she blankets her inheritance, she wonders whether she can ward off the possibility of its return:

> Now there is no scream. Once there was one and it settled slowly down to earth one hot summer afternoon; or did it float up, into that dark, too dark, blue sky? But surely it has gone away, forever.

Surely begs the question of its return; the seeming permanence lingers within and without, driving the child forever from her mother.

Bishop's child-speaker wanders from dwelling to dwelling, attempting to find an appropriate setting in which to articulate the elusive language of home. In spite of the relative comfort and security of her grandmother's (or aunt's) house, her dialogic narrative reveals an undercurrent of uncertainty. Home in Bishop's landscape becomes a metaphor for the instability not only of the human condition but of the dissonant structure of representation in language. Even the sturdiest nouns are subject to the flux of process: "Land lies in water," as she notes in "The Map." Part of the answer to the question of inscrutability lies in the age and relation of her primary caretakers during these youngest years: her grandparents.

Unlike the jovial grandfather (from "In the Village," "Gwendolyn," and "Manners"), the grandmother occupies a central role as life model for the child. When the deranged mother returns to the village, it is with the grandmother that her child has taken refuge. The grandmother assumes motherly duties, but cannot provide the chronological and generational link. She orchestrates the child's development from the remove of another generation. She must reach across the procreative years from a position of age and wisdom to counsel the child. Unlike a maternal presence, the grandmother lives in the suspended world familiar to us from "Sestina." While she unwittingly guides this child by her wisdom, she carries with it the tone of an acceptance of death. As the childhood takes shape, it assumes a form derived from the quality and character of the many re-experienced kitchen interludes. The almanaclike inevitability sheds tears of sorrow over these meetings.

Bishop recalls these scenes at approximately the same point each time, a point of maximum domesticity:

> My grandmother and I are alone again in the kitchen. We are talking.

Despite the present-tense the narrative generates a brooding tone, acknowledging the painful weight of the past and the uncertainty of the future. Death dominates the oppressive atmosphere. The inquisitive child probes. "Why, Gammy?" Even as the grandmother repeatedly attempts to answer, her tears choke back the truth. In the grandmother's world, the quotidian is sustained primarily by those daily activities that prepare us for death. The tropes of childhood, future, and hope cannot function properly in this atmosphere. Because the child, knowing no better, attempts to adapt to this world, she is unable to escape the almanac's injunction to "plant tears." Like the scream hanging over the village, these tears exist solely as release; the growth of knowledge and wisdom lies in the investment of emotion. The child sees the "liquid truth" permeate her world:

> My grandmother is sitting in the kitchen stirring potato mash for tomorrow's bread and crying into it. She gives me a spoonful and it tastes wonderful but wrong. In it I think I taste my grandmother's tears; then I kiss her and taste them on her cheek.

In "Memories of Uncle Neddy," as the grandmother rests secure in her role as family historian, her tears become a way of knowing the child's family and self:

> Then she [the grandmother] would start rocking, groaning and rocking, wiping her eyes with the edge of her apron, uttering from time to time the mysterious remark that was a sort of chorus in our lives: "Nobody knows . . . *nobody knows* . . ." I often wondered what my grandmother knew that none of the rest of us knew . . .
>
> [CPr, 241]

The child persists, plagued by the knowledge suspended between generations:

> I even asked her, "*What* do you know, Gammie, that we don't know? Why don't you tell us? Tell me!" She only laughed, dabbing at her tears. She laughed as easily as she cried, and one very often turned into the other (a trait her children and grandchildren inherited).

For the grandmother in "Uncle Neddy" specific knowledge no longer seems tied to the present. Every occurrence has its correlative. Each experience brings a tide of remembered associations. The grandfather, preferring to dismiss past unpleasantness and live in the congenial present, is abruptly dismissed by his wife:

> "*You'd* never remember anything. But *I* won't forget. *I* won't forget." And she set the rocking chair rocking as if it were, as it probably was, a memory machine.

Though she assumes the status of a repository of wisdom, the grandmother seems unable to share it. Her knowledge, limited by her own language of selfhood, domesticity, and expectations, remains bracketed by the period of her own childhood and early maturity. These stories explore the most debilitating effect of the generational hiatus: the fracturing of the tribal language. Without anyone to speak the language of early adulthood, this motherless home has lost the vitality to link succeeding generations.

In these works Bishop explores a language adequate to the world of childhood alienation, flight, fancy, tears, and humor. Investigating tentative tropes of socialization and self-awareness empowers the advancement of the child's language-apprehension and enlarges the child's knowable (that is, namable) universe. With these struggles for self-discovery Bishop engages the reader's sympathy and empathy. The process of troping, frankly exposed, schematizes the world, rendering it intellectually and emotionally digestible without contorting it to suit the eccentricities of a single, privileged life. Her child-self will go forth to reshape, and compensate for, her faulty inheritance, her lack of a suitable language of family. Subsequent individuation through language will invent a very different child, able to live and thrive in the flux between the known and the unknowable.

CHAPTER 4

The Childish Dusk

As the previous chapter demonstrates, much of the discovered rhetoric of identity derives from the act of giving voice to inheritance. A language of self-awareness derives, at least in the early stages, not so much from voicing interiority as from received knowledge. In continuing the concern of the previous chapter with Bishop's writing about childhood, this will trace the child's drive for independence through the partial integration of languages of exteriority and interiority. As Bishop's child-persona struggles to assemble the confusingly diverse particulars — the "elements" — of her world, her childhood gradually reveals itself as troping upon the poetic process itself. Whether as the child coveting Gwendolyn's blocks of "clear reds, yellows, and blues" or in the child's fight to obtain what Dickinson called "consent of language" in hopes of understanding her earth, Bishop strives to integrate the social and the individual hues of language, and to communicate the burden of this growing consciousness. The child's quest for linguistic connections between herself and others (what William James called "thought stuff and thing stuff" and what Henry James called "a collection of images and echoes to which meanings were attachable") establishes the terms of this chapter.

As the child-poet's horizons expand correspondingly to her literate explorations, she discovers how language divorced from experience can lead only to fearful confusions. Her attempt to find clarity in language incites speculation upon the similar nature of the poet's daily challenge. Even the child's misunderstandings, misadventures with the language, advance her cause for independence. One powerful source of this advancement is a strategy that is a hallmark of both Bishop's poetry and her stories: her adroit use of simile. She finds a particular use for the simile in these childhood pieces. Not only does this figurative device approximate the child's quest for integration in her world (supplying a means of fitting the pieces together), but it mirrors the poet's method of reaching and seeing through extension of her available language-hoard. The simile, like other forms of metaphor but more transparently, enables the poet to tap the reader's consciousness and memory in a way not otherwise possible.

What Bishop would later forsake—those "old correspondences" littering the bight—she enthusiastically endorses in text and strategy in her writings on childhood. Language, with its seemingly limitless power to reach into the world's unknown and untold resources, provides the child with a sense of control over her world and her knowledge. Even those momentary confusions of the tongue confer that "sense of privacy and power." Within the world of private meanings lies the child's analogic structure. Like the poet who heard Florida as "the state with the prettiest name" and saw it populated with "S-shaped birds" (CP, 32), the child clings to the surface (shape and length) and the sound of words; so many of the confusions (heard or seen) are as illuminating as the true vocabulary. Like James's Maisie, Bishop's child finds in "her mind a collection of images and echoes to which meanings are attachable." With this attachable diction she constructs a language-framework inside of which to function.

As the poet must relinquish her role as witness, abandoning her "infant sight" in favor of its metaphoric equivalent, its reconstruction as rhetoric, so must the child continually challenge her role as mere spectator, laying claim through language-awareness to a version of the world. What becomes essential to her growth is verifiable knowledge, which she can test for reliability and certainty. In the way that the child of "In the Village" learns to discriminate between varieties of candy by their effects (regarding her mother's favorite, Humbugs, the child proclaims with great certainty: "They last a long time, but lack the spit-producing brilliance of cherry or strawberry."), she learns to assess her widening circle of diction.

Being precocious and encircled by agéd relatives, the child naturally hears more than she can apprehend, process, or understand. This condition is further compounded by the fact that despite the oppressive presence of these adults many of these discoveries are independent of supervision. The poet, however, assumes a function as overbearing as any elderly relative, and invests the fictionally reconstituted child with a sensitivity to the sound and the meaning of words that in childhood she could not have voiced.

The shrill, suspended atmosphere of "In the Village" taints the environment itself; here the child cannot encounter words in isolation without a suffocating sense of loss. She overhears an adult discussion of places and possessions; she translates: "Vault. Awful word." The leaden monosyllable carries with it the association of her mother's belongings stored in a Boston bank vault. The mother, the scream, the threat become cruel possessors of that word, which is weighted by the legacy of death. The tale is one of black and white contrasts; and in that harsh light of absolutes the child gropes for an adequate language. Instinctively she stresses her interpretive store, hoping to make connections between the known and the unknown aspects of the environment, between her experience and her inadequate means of expression. In finding the word lies the key to comprehension. If only the child could attach meaning to this plague-ridden scene. Trapped, she searches for a pattern of knowing, a means of breaking the adult code:

> The clothes were black, or white, or black-and-white.
>
> "Here's a mourning hat," says my grandmother, holding up something large, sheer, and black, with large black roses on it; at least I guess they are roses, even if black.
>
> "There's that mourning coat she got the first winter," says my aunt.
>
> But always I think they are saying "morning." Why, in the morning, did one put on black? How early in the morning did one begin? Before the sun came up?
>
> [CPr, 254]

The homonymic confusions perplex the child. She associates familiar colors, black and white, with the blackness of Nate's blacksmith shop, its "tub of night-black water . . . by the forge," Nate's attire, and Nate's companion, a Newfoundland dog. She supplies associations for the colors, but fails to adequately enlarge her sense of relationships. She hears that familiar word mourning/morning, but questions without resolving its context. The child cannot conquer an unwitting ignorance, but perceives the disparity between what she knows and what she hears. She attempts to explain this within a limited range of language and experience. Blackness she easily associates with darkness. Does mourning attire mimic the night-blackness of Nate's? She yearns for the ability to test with cer-tainty—like the proof-positive spit-production of the candies at Mealy's. Momentarily she seems left without the satisfaction of such verifiable proof; but Bishop recalls this dissatisfaction as a necessary step to learning.

The child finds an opportunity to make the connection (however false) for herself. A family photograph album triggers the dis-covery:

> "Mrs. Miles . . ."
> "Mrs. Miles' spongecake . . ."
> "She was very fond of her."
> Another photograph—"Oh, that *Negro* girl! That friend."
> "She went to be a medical missionary. She had a letter from her, last winter. From Africa."
> "They were great friends."
> They show me the picture. She, too, is black-and-white, with glasses on a chain. A morning friend.

Her ability to confront the absence of knowledge provides a mo-mentary stay against confusion, a respite in which to consolidate gains.

Linguistic confusion seems ponderous in "In the Village," but in "Memories of Uncle Neddy," Bishop probes the child's misunder-standings in a more humorous way. She recalls daily auditory mis-hearings of her grandfather's mealtime prayer. As he recited, head bowed, "Oh Lord . . . we have reasons to thank Thee," the child auditor heard "raisins." Bishop suggests that this mishearing (with its undertone of deliberate misappropriation) is a condition of youth, a fault of ignorance and inattention. To further demon-strate, she supplies an even more grotesque mishearing:

> (But then, at this time I also confused "as we forgive our debtors" with "taters," a word I'd heard used humorously for "potatoes.")

[CPr, 231]

This is not to say that the child's world is entirely shaped by misinterpretation. Throughout the writings sounds the exuberance of a child who has begun to challenge the confines of experiential knowledge, who has begun to truly understand. This child, introduced as one who studies, learns, and knows, discerns those moments when her knowledge is sufficient to the task at hand. She dismisses misleading complexities with certainty; as she says, "We are in the 'Maritimes' but all that means is that we live by the sea." There is no confusion in her unease with the term *little girl*; she knows very well that it refers to Gwendolyn, her opposite. When the child examines her grandmother's crazy quilt and proclaims "I could read well enough to make out the names of the people I knew," she suggests an indissoluble bond between knowledge and experience. Hearing, sounding, and articulating are not enough; the child must be able to contain and empower her experience through language. The inability to do so will lead to such dislocations as the *mise en scène* of "In the Waiting Room."

In dramatizing the child's struggle to free herself, Bishop reveals an inescapable dependence upon adult experience and knowledge. Though the child bravely attempts to delineate this assemblage of "thing stuff" and "thought-stuff," she is limited by the poverty of her experience, even as she is threatened by the immediacy of her life. The adult world of "In the Village" with shrill incomprehensibility puts the child under stress, alienating her until she considers forsaking human society entirely:

> For a while I entertain the idea of not going home today at all, of staying safely here in the pasture all day, playing in the brook and climbing on the squishy, moss-covered hummocks in the swampy part. But an immense, sibilant, glistening loneliness suddenly faces me, and the cows are moving off to the shade of the fir trees, their bells chiming softly, individually.
>
> [CPr, 265]

No safety lies in the world of the pasture; the cows move off with their own kind into the firs (even as their artistic expression, the bells, sound "individually"), while the child must connect with her world through language and develop those similarities that make us all just one. Pastoralism offers no solace to a child eager to claim a place in an articulate world.

*

The spontaneity that Bishop attributes to Marianne Moore infuses her own writing as well. Part of her ability to capture the associative learning process of childhood lies in the shrewd application of the yoking potential of the simile. In portraiture-through-simile she depicts not only the child's world (as she links known with the unknown), but exposes her commitment as adult poet to the remembered and reconstructed world of the child. While as the child attempts to describe the place of the strange or uncanny in her world, Bishop counters that clumsiness with her mature and canny skill.

Lacking the relative security of position or place, the child draws inspiration and confidence from those who possess that security. These supporting inhabitants linger in the poetry not merely because of their visual clarity, but because of their spiritual and richly allusive qualities. Depicting these characters depicts the epicenter of the child's world, so that further examination of the poetics of childhood requires attention to the supporting network of those who people the village.

When Bishop questions the source of Moore's gift for simile, she attributes it to her ability to "give herself up entirely to the object under contemplation, to feel in all sincerity how it is to be *it*." Yet viewing Bishop's portraits exposes a calculated process, a set of strategies deliberately revealed. Her tentative assemblage of the child's world shows how she constructs her universe; the constellations are plotted along individual points, making the whole figure intelligible to the child-creator. The child knits her knowledge and experience into the fabric of the moment. Her observations illustrate less about Mealy, Mr. Johnson, or Nate, and more about the observer who seeks to explain—or place—those who people her village. Her attempts to position and place these figures parallels her own desire to secure her place in life. The living, animal and human, are located by their respective roles and their places of work. In this way, the child draws upon all her resources, environmental and intellectual, to explain her world with this relational strategy. Reviewing some of these childhood portraits reveals a child not merely reaching out into her world of reference but reinventing that world in relation to herself.

The most extended cast of child-constructed portraits belongs to

"In the Village." Here the child's selection and depiction of her surrounding world purports to speak for itself. This selection and portrayal challenges as well as defines the domestic world. The narrative depicts surrounding people—grandparents, blacksmith, and others—by their roles, occupations, and places of work. The child reaches out of her books into the present tense, hoping to find associative clues to the identities of those around her. The dressmaker, for example, is "crawling around and around on her knees eating pins as Nebuchadnezzar had crawled eating grass." The child draws upon those "gilded red or green books, unlovely books, filled with bright new illustrations of the Bible stories," and straddles the worlds of books and the quotidian, groping for the words to confirm her and their existence. She mentions "broad and fat" Mealy of the candy store, who "looks as though she and the counter and showcase, stuffed dimly with things every which way, were settling down together out of sight." The post office, too, assumes identity through resemblance—"inside it looked as chewed as a horse's manger." The search for likeness approximates the child's quest for identity. Yet even as she affixes these figures, she turns to others for asylum, sketching, for example, the most memorable scene of person and place in the figure and environment of Nate the blacksmith.

Nate is the counterforce to the child's disturbed family life; the "beautiful pure sound" of his purposeful creation cancels her mother's scream of formless despair. Unlike the black-and-white mourning of her home, the radiant blackness of this blacksmith's nether world illuminates the child's life. Here she meets the elemental world of particulars, fragments waiting to be assimilated. Unlike the candy store and post office, the blacksmith shop finds its value and empowerment in the realm of myth. Nate in all his blackness is less important than his world, his creations, and his attendant Newfoundland and horse. Nate is that rare example of a self-creation that requires no figurative language to confirm its presence. As the child declares, "Nate was there." Nate himself illuminates a straightforward delineation of his blackness, his otherness:

> Nate, wearing a long black leather apron over his trousers and
> bare chest, sweating hard, a black leather cap on top of dry,

> thick, black-and-gray curls, a black sooty face; iron filings,
> whiskers, and gold teeth, all together, and a smell of red-hot
> metal and horses' hoofs.

Composed of the salt of manly sweat, and sprinkled with the iron
filings of his trade, Nate embodies "the elements speaking." If the
child discovers childhood anywhere in this story, she finds it at
Nate's, where an elemental mode of being, almost prelinguistic,
prevails.

The effect of the scream, on the other hand, is atavistic in another way, and wars with Nate's elemental artistry:

> *Clang.*
> The pure note: pure and angelic.
> The dress was all wrong. She screamed.
> The child vanishes.

Onomatopoeia, followed respectively by narrative from her mother's, then from the third-person narrator's points-of-view, closes
with a stage direction. This linguistic showiness, having exhausted
the resources of the child's language, signals the climax of the
story.

The discordant, unpredictable scream destroys the child, displaces her. Yet she finds another self, the child self, in the reverse-
image heaven of Nate's shop. This seemingly negative environment
challenges her to draw more firmly her associative world. In the
"black and glittering dust" of the smithy, objects and apparitions
can be made to be what they seem. Shadows give shape to the
material world. The child's ability to yoke disparate images even
creates an alternative galaxy:

> A tub of night-black water stands by the forge. The horseshoes
> sail through the dark like bloody little moons and follow each
> other like bloody little moons to drown in the black water, hiss-
> ing, protesting.

Here Bishop mingles the child's perception with the artist's reitera-
tion and the adult's moral re-interpretation. Nate's horseshoes have
lives of their own, and defy their creator and their destiny. While
Nate occupies the center of this wonder-working providence, he is
comfortably flanked by his approving friendly beasts:

> Inside, the bellows creak. Nate does wonders with both hands; with one hand. The attendant horse stamps his foot and nods his head as if agreeing to a peace treaty.

The concluding simile betrays the presence of the adult narrator, and points to the singlehandedness of these wonders, which in turn mimic Nate's singlemindedness, his simplicity. Part of his elemental grandeur consists of no more than his simplicity, which is monumental. Positioning herself in Nate's world, explaining it to herself, affects the child's view of the discord without: "Now it is settling down, the scream." The peace treaty takes effect between the house and the blacksmith shop.

Yet, central as Nate's world is to the child, Bishop reserves the grandest exposition for the recipient of Nate's talents, the horse he is shoeing. Perhaps the child sees herself in the horse, another "real guest." Indeed, this horse seems a vehicle of transport to another world:

> His harness hangs loose like a man's suspenders . . . Manure piles up behind him, suddenly, neatly. He, too, is very much at home. He is enormous. His rump is like a brown, glossy globe of the whole brown world. His ears are secret entrances to the underworld. His nose is supposed to feel like velvet and does, with ink spots under milk all over its pink.

Here the artist-narrator works on the child's perception, adding an erotic aura in the description of the horse's rump, and a linguistic sophistication in the alliteration ("glossy globe") and internal rhyme ("milk," "ink," "pink"). The child experiences the horse as she could never experience anything at home. The horse seems unrestrained by the manlike trappings (his harness); he represents, in the eyes of the child, the earth itself. In this steed, the child sees openings to the other worlds, perhaps even other times. If Nate's shop represents a shadowy asylum, the horse suggests the possibility of escape from the village entirely.

As the child reaches out to grasp for likeness in her world, she struggles to assemble the particulars of her life to gain a larger grasp of existence. Nate's blacksmith shop, with its monumental figures and clear alternative to domestic failure, offers her an opportunity to imagine a more sufficient world. Assembling this world from the audible and tactile elements at hand calls forth her gift for metaphor, which is her primary linguistic means of self-integration. In her attempts to explain to herself the wonder of those who people the blacksmith shop she initiates a process of self-education through the expansion of her rhetorical ability. The child gains in independence as well as imagery by mastering fresh perceptions with available language.

Nate's purposeful world, the one that most fruitfully yields to the child's quest for correspondences, defeats the chaotic, ever-encroaching world of insanity and discord. Derived from and forever tethered to the enriching physicality of this earth, Nate's audible clarity, however momentarily, cancels the chaos about the child:

> *Clang.*
> And everything except the river holds its breath.
> Now there is no scream. Once there was one and it settled slowly down to earth one hot summer afternoon; or did it float up, into that dark, too dark, blue sky? But surely it has gone away, forever.

The adult's globalizing of inner experience is followed by the child's wondering voice, in turn answered by the adult writer. The child's concern grows from a fear that her knowledge is incomplete; though she hopes that this new world will keep the confusions at home at bay, she feels recurrent danger. "Surely" and "forever" are verbal clues to her hopeful anxiety.

Bishop's childhood writings seek to recover the process of toddler intellection. Bishop bridges the gap between experience and reason, allowing her tales to teeter on the brink—of the age of seven. This poetic linkage is a strategy central to her writings: a belief in the journey, not the destination. A tentative timetable of moments and miles fashions these recreations; only the journey can be shared.

Bishop's childhood provides a curious opportunity to examine and construct a source for her self and her writing. As she reaches backward across her life, she delves into the psychic source of her work. In "First Death in Nova Scotia" [QT], Bishop continues her childhood confrontations; but this child meets death, not her past but the moment itself. Not interested in the final encounter of some "imperishable autumn," Bishop re-enacts, re-experiences a child's first encounter with death, its significance and its rituals. In this translation from the moment to the poem, the poet has performed what Clifford Geertz, in his essay "Blurred Genres: The Refiguration of Social Thought," would call the shift from "the *saying*" to "the *said*" so that "its meaning can persist in a way its actuality cannot." "First Death" resists the temptation to make all remembrance clouded by the death-filled past. The child's life must be made palpable to dramatize the lessons of this poem. Once again, this is a poem of language-knowledge: how a child depicts death through yoking familiar images, how adults present the fact through historical reconstruction.

The heavy Edwardian decor seems homey and comfortable, yet unlike the setting of "In the Village," this is a *nature morte*. The struggle to comprehend leads the child to the familiar, "understood" objects as means to interpretation. Watching her mother lay out her cousin, the child is inspired by the presence and proximity of another victim chilled by death: "a stuffed loon / shot and stuffed by Uncle / Arthur." Struck dumb by Arthur's bullet, the loon has borne silent witness to the parlor proceedings. The bird shares the child's view:

> Arthur's coffin was
> a little frosted cake,
> and the red-eyed loon eyed it
> from his white, frozen lake.

[CP, 125]

Here Bishop manipulates her scale, till the coffin is smaller than the bird, so that the latter might eye it as he would a piece of cake. Yet "the . . . lake" is enlarged to the size of a big pond. This gives the poem a disturbing effect of dislocation.

The posed objects cluttering the room—the loon, the royal couples in chromographs, Arthur, the doll-like corpse (reminiscent of Gwendolyn)—are all frozen in death. The child's quest forces her to reposition her dead cousin, placing him within her immediate frame of reference.

> Arthur was very small.
> He was all white, like a doll
> that hadn't been painted yet.

> Jack Frost had started to paint him
> the way he always painted
> the Maple Leaf (Forever).
> He had just begun on his hair,
> a few red strokes, and then
> Jack Frost had dropped the brush
> and left him white, forever.

The second and third lines show Bishop's use of reduction and her struggle for mastery of information by simile. In the fourth, fifth, and sixth lines she associates the Canadian national emblem with the myth of Jack Frost, then follows that by extrapolating Frost to her one myth about Arthur.

Bishop has sought to put the child in charge of her learning. She attempts to move beyond the realm of received knowledge and understand the process of death itself. As she had used Uncle Arthur's stuffed loon as analogue to her coffined cousin, so will she use that seasonal agent, Jack Frost, to explain in her terms the transformation of Cousin Arthur.

A child's translation of death through reduction and imagination is also the subject of Emily Dickinson's "I noticed People disappeared":

> I noticed People disappeared
> When but a little child —
> Supposed they visited remote
> Or settled Regions wild —
> Now know I — They both visited
> And settled Regions wild
> But did because they died
> A Fact withheld the little child —

Dickinson's poem fixes on one of Bishop's overwhelming concerns, "the facts withheld." No one attempts to communicate with this child and make the ritual of death an acceptable experience. The child is talked at — "Come and say goodbye / to your little cousin Arthur" — but remains speechless, as if aware of the futility of asking questions of those unaware of the troubling confusions of death. Forever remaining the possession of a crippled childhood, this memory hangs cryogenically suspended in the death-chill of that "cold, cold parlor."

For Bishop, childhood is less a matter of what happened and more a concern with perceiving and interpreting occurrences. Consequently, she prefers to keep her child in control, isolated from the adult world — and even less from her mature self. Even as Bishop's grandparents instruct, the child questions and discovers independently. The process of childhood discovery becomes a key element in these writings. Though most of the family pieces cluster about her grandmother, the poem "Manners (For a Child of 1918)" [QT] and the prose story "Gwendolyn" illustrate the girl's relationship with her grandfather.

The gentle ballad stanzas of "Manners" provide more than a child's view of the "ways" of the adult world: they release us from the resonant and intimidating conclusion of "In the Village." In this journey with her grandfather, the child assumes behavior soon to be expected in the rational years of the future. The elder's instructions counterpoint the undercurrent of the child's doubts and worries. She matches the instructions to experience, hoping to find some congruence.

Surely the most powerful union of child and grandfather, however, is in the story "Gwendolyn." A postfuneral graveyard scene draws young and old to the family plot. The activities of routine upkeep encompass the place and tradition and purpose. As Bishop fears, mere mention of names is not enough to make her memories significant. She must make more of this meeting than genealogy; she must discover something. So, as in "Manners," the events are simultaneous but separate. Even as her grandfather rhythmically "scythed away, and talked . . . haphazardly about the people lying there," the child proceeds to discover and assimilate on her own. In a setting suitable for a tale by Brothers Grimm, the child pieces together her experience of the place, and of death. She will not reach beyond and link herself to her grandfather's generation; her viewpoint remains that of a child:

> A few plots were lightly chained in, like the Presbyterian church,
> or fenced in with wood or iron, like little gardens . . .

She familiarizes herself with the place through association with other known places. Though she manages to tame the graveyard, she retains a living fear:

> Blueberries grew there, too, but I didn't eat them, because I felt I
> "never knew," as people said . . .

The child has every reason to fear this place of death, but her
grandmother knows no such fear. For her elders, death has become just another fact, since everyone is destined to nourish the
berries.

Even as the grandfather drones on about the buried relatives,
the child relates to the children's graves, attempting to place herself
in relation to the prematurely departed ones. She seems most anxious to retrieve their identities, their earthly significance; in this
way, she translates their lives:

> I was, of course, particularly interested in the children's graves,
> their names, what ages they had died at — whether they were older
> than I or younger.

The memorial markers are of particular interest, the last evidence
of a person, the final means of placing and naming the individual.
Even as the child plays about the "little lambs," caressing them and
sitting upon them, she senses the encroachment of oblivion, which
is even worse than death. Soon even these final markers will yield
to the lichen, "the long grass and roses and blueberries and teaber-
ries." The processional chain of vegetation suggests an organic
rightness to this fate of sheer obliteration.

Not merely content to revisit faded memories, Bishop seeks to
discover new paths to knowledge. Childhood becomes less a scrap-
book of faded times and more a laboratory to examine process
and discovery. She must discover the origins of that Emersonian
journey from the particular to the whole. Like the Williams of
Paterson, she embarks

> To make a start
> out of particulars
> and make them general, rolling
> up the sum, by defective means . . .

Bishop must penetrate what Robert Lowell perceived as the "rock-
like" surface of childhood, revealing that universal core, a pathway
to knowledge. Certain in her truth of childhood, Bishop knows the

essential nature of the "separateness" of childhood; in that separate identity lies the mystery and magic of that age. Childhood is a world apart.

Like the dreamy divigations of the grandparents in Bishop's "The Moose," the graveyard scenes of "Gwendolyn" (like those of Lowell's "Dunbarton") unite life's extremities, age and youth. The child circumvents the troubling parental generation and finds security in that apparently untroubled age of her grandparents. The trajectory of her growing knowledge reverses from the grandparental "world of light" to the origin that is "dark, salt, clear, moving, utterly free," and utterly unattainable without embracing oblivion.

"Memories of Uncle Neddy" seems to draw inspiration in both form and content from Lowell's "91 Revere Street." Bishop subjects herself to a self-prescribed test of "significance" and "assurance." This time instead of Uncle Artie, she recalls her Uncle Neddy. This memoir illustrates how different the strategies and purposes of this reminiscence are from the childhood set pieces.

As Lowell begins his "autobiographical fragments" with a place (91 Revere Street), a person (Major Mordecai Myers), Bishop begins her memories with present-day Rio de Janeiro: "Uncle Neddy, that is his, [her] Uncle Edward," and the arrival of his likeness:

> But here he is again now, young and clean, about twelve years old, with nothing between us but a glaze of old-fashioned varnishing. His widow, Aunt Hat, sent him to me, shipped him thousands of miles from Nova Scotia, along with one of his younger sisters, my mother, in one big crate. Why on earth did Aunt Hat send me the portrait of her late husband? My mother's might have been expected, but Uncle Neddy's came as a complete surprise; and now I can't stop thinking about him.
>
> [CPr, 229]

Lowell's family portrait leads into a tale of the outsider. Who could be more alien in his Mayflower world than the Jewish Mordecai Myers? "Uncle Neddy," on the other hand, provides Bishop with an opportunity to examine and reveal from a pictorial vantage point those missing years between grandparents and self; like Lowell's Major Myers, Neddy is a kind of family outcast. As Bishop reverses the linear perspective of the painting, the world of her uncle assumes perceptible scale and dimension. She discovers the "ancestor-children" in a cascade of memories, told and retold. Bishop, like her remembered relative, becomes a product of both memory and life. The narrative shifts from the dramatic depiction of a child's discoveries, inching toward awareness, to a meditative assemblage of drifting focal points: "I remember only now," "I remember his telling me," "How often did my grandmother tell me," "I got the impression later," "My own recollections begin now, things I saw or heard." Bishop works within a fluid time frame within which *then* and *now* become tides of the individual life span. Breaking with her past, she attempts to make the specific characteristics of a family member, the individual traits and triumphs, "significant" to the outsider. Rumors and recollections bolster the person into being, but finally these "memories" collapse into antiquarian irrelevance.

Deprived of the invigorating presence of Bishop's "Elsewhere" writings, "Memories of Uncle Neddy" brings little more than knowledge of Edwardian Nova Scotia, a world of overstuffed furniture, tinware, chromographs, and "hair-cloth-and-mahogony northern parlor[s]." The story lacks the presence of a persona as vivid as the child of "In the Village," and needs someone to discern the importance of perspective in impressions. The dusty darkness of the remembered tin shop lacks the seductive qualities of Nate's. Once again Bishop seeks to visualize and particularize through similes, but though they are perceptually vivid they convey no feeling. The "dull lengths of stove pipe with wrinkled blue joints like elephants' legs dangling over" (reminiscent of Stevens's "elephant-colorings of tires") and the "stove-lid lifters hanging up in a bunch, like dried herbs" reveal the prosaic world of Bishop. Not only did Bishop use the simile to approximate the child's quest for associative knowledge, but she compressed and energized her poetry in so doing. The particulars weight these memories unnecessarily and fail to generate the dramatically powerful variety of relational complexities Lowell engenders in *91 Revere Street*. The relative failure of this reminiscence demonstrates how essential a language of remove is to Bishop's writing. Yet this memoir provided Bishop with the opportunity to frankly address her generational superiors, to momently catch for examination certain images "like breath on a mirror." As Bishop concludes:

> The last time I saw him he was very weak and very bent. The eyes of the man who used to lean down to hug and kiss me were now on a level with mine.

This new perspective, clearly delineated here, finally frees the speaker of the child's limitations and allows her to look squarely, eye to eye, at the world of the adult.

CHAPTER 5

Native Knowledge

The world of the adult, even more than that of the child, is beguiling but unsettlingly diverse. Though most comfortable generating poetry from domestic images of her childhood, Bishop, like other perceptive people, was drawn to subjects, images of people and landscapes, language, and themes best defined by their otherness. How she explores this material, and the problem of why her poetry about African-American and Brazilian folk life compares poorly to her portraits of North American ancestral provincials are the issues of this chapter. From the perspective of her mastery of the conventions of English-language poetry, Bishop re-invents herself in an alien context. Working from romantic–modern traditions and expectations established by Wordsworth, Emerson, Hopkins, Williams, and Frost, including the re-invigoration of the pastoral mode, she attempts to advance her grasp of dailiness to illustrate, if not penetrate, aspects of culture from which she remains emotionally estranged. She juxtaposes familiar cultural images and constructs with those of the exotic cultures of Key West and Brazil, and, in the process, generates tropes of self-realization in which she herself becomes "more truly and more strange." She becomes an "experience-distant" fieldworker attempting to illuminate what Clifford Geertz has called "concepts that, for another people, are experience-near."

Bishop eventually reverses interior and anterior stances and learns to see herself as an alien (as the section titles of *Questions of*

102

Travel suggest), a perpetual guest. The self-realization, however, earned in the struggle with an unmoored childhood and migratory adulthood furthers that quest for the fully grasped moment, which would be accomplished only in "Crusoe in England." The challenge of these poems of provincial relocation, as with much of her work, is to transcend romantic conventions of the picturesque and the sublime and exact a language adequate to reconstitute, in a deconstructive landscape, a viable self-realization. Yet like Adrienne Rich's attempt to identify herself with an American slave (see "From an Old House in America"), Bishop's gestures would often be troubled by what Aldon Nielsen in *Reading Race* has labeled "presumptive identification[s]" with the "racial other."

Tropes of family life dominate Bishop's childhood world. Specifically, a familiar language defines a relational structure for the child to grow within, and serves as a means (if not *the* means) for the child to reach out into a greater society and secure a place in the world. The family can absorb a great many shocks to its structure and sincerity and still offer both place and name to the child. Bishop, however, lacked this initial orientation, which may account for her desire for a language of transparent simplicity, a rhetorical grasp of temporal surfaces. Like her "unknown bird" and "little dog," she appears at times to be waiting patiently for those direct answers. The exotic settings of Key West and Brazil expand her search for a language of utter sufficiency through examination of unfamiliar particulars, but she risks imposing her own desire for a restorative simplicity upon her subjects.

Poems like "Jerónimo's House," "Faustina, or Rock Roses," and "Songs for a Colored Singer" — portraits of, or poems in the voices of, the "homely folk" — defer Bishop's urge to "drive to the interior," to accomplish a fuller autobiographical grasp of her familiar world. Despite her interest in folk art and music (she was intrigued by Brazilian sambas), Bishop rejected the apparent aesthetic simplicity and familial security of folk life, in part because these too readily evoked the conventional tropes of the romantic picturesque. Consequently, however, her portraits of people in unfamiliar cultures (defined by separate linguistic communities), straining against her intellect and marred by cultural deafness, resemble her "Florida" alligator: "who has five distinct calls: / friendliness, love, mating, war, and a warning." The provincial outlook seems to her to deny the imperative to invent means of expression adequate to the complexities of her life. Even the child-poet of "In the Waiting Room" understands the need to learn from experience, to name its intersections with the interior world and name the present in a diction and rhetoric that firmly links it to the past and the future. The present tense, if divorced from a grasp of the past, is a refuge forbidden to her.

If all the shifts of place in Bishop's childhood made her feel like a perpetual guest, life abroad would impose on her the role of expatriate, or perpetual tourist. Mocking this uneasy status, "Arrival at Santos" [QT] asks:

> . . . Oh, tourist,
> is this how this country is going to answer you
>
> and your immodest demands for a different world,
> and a better life, and complete comprehension
> of both at last, and immediately,
> after eighteen days of suspension?

[CP, 89]

Bishop is properly skeptical of her abilities to accommodate herself to this new world. Like the halves of *Questions of Travel*—"Brazil" and "Elsewhere" (inverting the expected designations of known and unknown)—these two worlds occupy unintegrated space, separated permanently by an eighteen-day oceanic hiatus. This distancing speaks to the difficulties of integrating these poems of differing northern and southern memory and experience. The lessons learned in the attempt constitute the wisdom of "Crusoe in England."

"Filling Station" [QT] offers a place to begin to delineate the problems of integrating unfamiliar or unavailable social and cultural milieus. A fussy feminine voice plots the scene. The poem moves from critique—"Oh, but it is dirty!"—to affirmation—"Somebody loves us all" without losing tone, as if to assert, despite its prissiness, its emotional range. Both assertions depend on the exaggeratedly finical persona-voice for recognition and clarification of the relationship between language-subject and object. The clarity of revelation requires the acceptance of the authority of this somewhat flighty voice.

The first stanza encounters this diminutive, dirty filling station with a tone of amused disgust. This unctuous station offers no clean surface on which to step, sit, or lean. The caretaker-narrator worries about the public welfare in this place of discarded lubricants. The place seems deserted, vaguely disturbing, alien, provincial.

The second stanza, however, introduces, or at least recognizes, the filling station family. Bishop had to delineate the oily surroundings before she could populate the station with presences that derive their identity in part from the obscuring power of the dirt and grease. Father in a "dirty, / oil-soaked monkey suit" and his "several quick and saucy / and greasy sons" compose the tribe. To underscore the masculine disarray, Bishop compresses judgment with depiction: "it's a family filling station, / all quite thoroughly dirty." The work environment begs for the tidying presence of a woman, a wife, or a mother. The station itself appears to be a resting place for men and dogs: the wicker furniture ("crushed and grease- / impregnated" and with a "dirty dog") offers that residential look. Bishop allows "grease-" to teeter at the end of the line, isolating and heightening the vaguely sexual connotations of "impregnated."

The descriptively self-contained stanzas of "Filling Station" cause it to resemble "Sestina" more than any other Bishop poem. The theatrical positioning of props and people echoes the dominant image patterns of the piece. At one step removed, we glimpse the touches of those present: "Some comic books provide / the only note of color"—and perhaps someone absent: "They [the comic books] lie / upon a big dim doily / draping a taboret / (part of the set), beside / a big hirsute begonia." Surely there can be no sense of intellectual presence, or for that matter, even craft. Bishop sees neither mind nor hand at work in the debris. Upon what then does the poem turn? Perhaps because of the orchestrating falsetto voice, the poem depends upon noting the absence of an actual feminine presence. It asks us to sense the former presence, then to miss, the decorator of the filling station. This note of nostalgia exploits conventional expectations: Domestic scenes—it is now clear that domesticity is the standard to which the narrator has held this scene—require a woman, a wife, a mother here, even as "Sestina" does.

A rhetorical cascade of questions suggests the extent of the narrator's tentatively withheld knowledge:

> Why the extraneous plant?
> Why the taboret?
> Why, oh why, the doily?
> (Embroidered in daisy stitch
> with marguerites, I think,
> and heavy with gray crochet.)
>
> [CP, 127–28]

The selective questioning and insider's conjectures (further empha-
sized by the parachesis of "gray crochet") link factual and speculative registers of awareness. The poem challenges the reader to offer
any explanation other than a woman's sometimes presence. No
longer the harsh *d*s of the beginning stanzas, the calming, lullaby-
like *w*s and *s*s of the oil cans sound a peaceful and reconciling
note as the poem drifts to a vaguely humorous and reassuring
conclusion:

> Somebody embroidered the doily.
> Somebody waters the plant,
> or oils it, maybe. Somebody
> arranges the rows of cans
> so that they softly say:
> ESSO – SO – SO – SO
> to high-strung automobiles.
> Somebody loves us all.

There is an understood presence, a nurturing and artistic overseer
to this otherwise casual business. It is on the care and the arrangement of objects that survival depends. The soft utterances of the
oil cans (pouring oil on the world's troubled waters) gently mock
and soothe the high-strung automobiles that so cruelly embody the
idea of cultural and social progress, a progress that has soiled this
microcosm without entirely civilizing it.

The decoding of alien messages occupies Bishop throughout
these poems of displacement and provinciality. Though these
poems generally avoid the familial unease of her Nova Scotia
poems, "Questions of Travel," which is a poem of no particularly
designated landscape but of landscapes in general, hints at unsatis-
fied childhood longings when she points out that it would have
been a pity:

—Not to have had to stop for gas and heard
the sad, two-noted, wooden tune
of disparate wooden clogs
carelessly clacking over
a grease-stained filling-station floor.

[CP, 94]

The sly disparagement of "wooden tune" and careless "clacking" teasingly reminds us that this is a poet's observation, not merely a hint of uncurbed nostalgia. Perhaps the same filling station served as inspiration, or perhaps the transference to native soil engendered the speculative, assured tone of "Filling Station." As Bishop struggles with a foreign world and consciousness, she discovers that what had once seemed childhood preoccupations now dominate her world and art.

Bishop's difficulties in writing successfully about unfamiliar cultures derive from her lack of relevant personal history. Despite her attempts to empower her poetry with aesthetic self-sufficiency, and although she avoids what Harold Bloom has called the trope of vulnerability, she is essentially an autobiographical writer. Consequently, it is difficult for her to fully empathize with a day-by-day existence informed by a lifetime's understanding of a place and culture alien to her own. The intensity of her most effective work requires a strong sense of landscape and experience; her strongest writing on life in Key West and Brazil, such as her memoir of Gregorio Valdes and the poem "Faustina," offer a vivid sense of landscape and atmosphere, but the lives of her characters, to some degree, elude her. Further, her poetic experience is unhelpful. English-language poetry offers no adequate model for empathizing with people so distinct from herself in culture and class background. Even a grimy work situation seems impenetrable except in terms with which she's already familiar.

In her Brazil and Key West writing, as if to accommodate herself to these Catholic Hispanic societies, Bishop attempts to deal with the greatest personal difference between herself and others: the presence of the family. In doing so, she violates a tradition that sees the solitary pastoral figure as the embodiment of the distinction between the intellect and the emotions, the spirit and the body. Whether represented by the brawn of Hopkins's "Harry Ploughman" ("amansstrength") or the inspirational fortitude of Wordsworth's leech-gatherer or the loneliness of Frost's "Hill Wife," the solitary provincial, isolated for examination, draws meaning from the emotional and intellectual investment of the poet. Bishop chooses to engage an alien sensibility and institution — simplicity and the family — in hopes that they will instruct her, infuse her with a knowledge seemingly forbidden by her early experience. Her engagement with provincial households, languages, and customs demonstrates that she is most successful when, like Hopkins, she sees the provincial as another intriguing part of the landscape.

In the memoir "Gregorio Valdes, 1879–1939" Bishop, deliberately forestalling the confrontation with ignorance, introduces Señor Valdes, a Cuban Key West painter, through his work. He thereby becomes a fellow artist, if, indeed, only a "folk" artist. The intersection of his life and Bishop's occurs not in the Key West, Florida, of 1939, but in the artistic representations of that shared world. Whether or not Bishop can understand the Valdes family life, she can surely judge his vision. As it coincides with her own, she finds access to the life itself.

A painting becomes an introduction:

> The first painting I saw by Gregorio Valdes was in the window
> of a barber-shop on Duval Street, the main street of Key West.
>
>   [CPr, 51]

The setting of the painting occasions a brief situating description of the neighborhood, justified at last with "It was a view, a real view." This view prompts relationships not only within the visual range, but also within the artistically historical purview. The "mysterious properties of perspective," says Bishop, seem one with those in Rousseau's *The Cariole of M. Juniot*. In fact, when Bishop decides to meet this fellow artist, she searched for physiognomic correspondences there as well:

> Gregorio was very small, thin and sickly, with a childish face and
> tired brown eyes — in fact he looked a little like the *Self-Portrait
> of El Greco*.

Bishop continues this matching process throughout this memorial tribute. She relies upon these connectives to remind us that this man, in the way he has lived his life and the way Bishop presents him, is both an artist and a work of art.

The correspondences are invoked not to portray the man, but rather to explore his art and his world in the context of Bishop's own. So, when the first commissioned painting is delivered by Gregorio, Bishop immediately situates it within her own "northern" experience:

> When he delivered this picture there was no one at home, so he left it on the verandah leaning against the wall. As I came home that evening I saw it there from a long way off down the street — a fair-sized copy of the house, in green and white, leaning against its green-and-white prototype. In the gray twilight they seemed to blur together and I had the feeling that if I came closer I would be able to see another miniature copy of the house leaning on the porch of the painted house, and so on — like the Old Dutch Cleanser advertisements.

Bishop then extends this method to Gregorio himself — seeing him in his habitat, his home being, as it were, the perfect reflection of a self as seen through his paintings. After an inventory of the home, Bishop links the man, his work, and his environment:

> The bareness of a Cuban house, and the apparent remoteness of every object in it from every other object, gives one the same sensation as the bareness and remoteness of Gregorio's best pictures.

Finally in his fatal illness, Gregorio requires an outside (that is, Hispanic) relationship. In his moribund state, Gregorio becomes "like one of those Mexican retablo paintings of miraculous cures, only in this case we were afraid no miraculous cure was possible."

Having claimed a place in Gregorio's world, Bishop relaxes into a postmortem retrospection of this man's family life. Not only was this of no concern to her while the painter lived, but these relations might have detracted from her own relationship with him. Bishop finds herself in the advantageous role of spectator. She sketches a life she never knew: that of a patriarch, his sons and daughters, and his grandchildren. Displaced by death and custom, she reflects on the integrity of this man she hardly knew. The anecdotes are offered as testimony to an artistic life; unable to do more than suggest this spiritual integration, Bishop ascribes much of Gregorio's beauty to mystery, "natural virtue." Dissatisfied with her tribute to the man, she closes with a displacing summary:

> Anyway, who could fail to enjoy and admire those secretive palm trees in their pink skies, the Traveler's Palm, like "the fan-filamented antenna of a certain gigantic moth . . ." or the picture of the church in Cuba copied from a liquor advertisement and labeled with so literal a translation from the Spanish, "Church of St. Mary Rosario 300 Years Constructed in Cuba."

The seemingly offhand dismissal—"Anyway"—testifies to Bishop's felt inability to dig more deeply into this alien life. Even as readers of Bishop are wise to depend upon her work rather than on critical or biographical commentaries, so she must valorize Gregorio's paintings as the authoritative source of knowledge about both the man and his art.

In discussing Valdes, Bishop allows herself a vantage point (strictly as an observer) and a subject (focusing comment and judgment on the paintings) congenial to her alien status. The peremptory conclusion acknowledges the limitations of her approach. Purporting to deal with the man, the essay, once it has established the priority of the art as the key to the man, concludes with a tacit acknowledgment that this conflation of art and artist is not quite enough.

Because art, landscape, and the domestic scene are congenial topics for Bishop, in writing about people with whom she lacks common cultural currency, she tends to identify them with their work or setting. As Valdes becomes his art, so in "Jerónimo's House" [NS], in adopting the persona of her subject, Bishop identifies him with his house. Her correspondence with Marianne Moore reveals that she originally planned this poem to be a tribute or at least a description of the house, not the owner:

> I am enclosing another poem that I'm afraid isn't very good—I just can't tell any more—perhaps if I think about your maxim for Key West I may be able to improve it in some way. I thought something *jiggeldy* would suit the Cuban houses, but I don't know. They pay from $1.00 to $2.00 a week rent . . . [February 19, 1940]

Though Bishop fails to itemize her reservations, her quest for something "jiggeldy" has undermined the poem by consigning it to the category of the unserious. Assuming an uncomfortable, provincial voice, more that of Bishop's letter than of her ostensible subject, the poem collapses under the strain of competing attitudes. Unlike his fellow artist, Gregorio Valdes, Jerónimo offers no opportunity for shared visions or experience. Bishop seems stranded, and, worse yet, repelled by this foreign experience. The tribute (originally the poem bore a dedication to José Marti) turns sour immediately. Comparing the opening stanza with a passage from a later work, "Santarém" (1978), illustrates how the same imagery can either serve or subvert a poem. In "Jerónimo's House," we are introduced to a self-made, perishable "palace":

> My house, my fairy
>   palace, is
> of perishable
>   clapboards with
> three rooms in all,
>   my gray wasps' nest
> of chewed-up paper
>   glued with spit.
>
> [CP, 34]

The metaphorical nest of "Chewed-up paper / glued with spit" rhymes, resting uneasily against the "perishable" palace. Neither the voice nor intelligence of these lines is credible. This is the voice of the tourist, not the lifelong resident. The home Bishop divines in the metaphor of the nest finally emerges in the late poem "Santarém":

> In the blue pharmacy the pharmacist
> had hung an empty wasps' nest from a shelf:
> small, exquisite, clean matte white,
> and hard as stucco. I admired it
> so much he gave it to me.
>
> [CP, 186]

Unlike the awkwardly organic, masticated, and spit-bound "nest" of "Jerónimo's House," this object grows in aesthetic distance. As with the "inscrutable house" of "Sestina," the significance rests in the foiled search. Chaste in its perfection — "small, exquisite, clean white matte, / and hard as stucco" — the nest takes on new life as an *objet trouvé* that Bishop invests with congenial qualities.

In "Jerónimo's House" all attempts at homeliness and homeyness ring false. Such attempts seem artificial to Bishop, who knows the necessity of relinquishing "infant sight." Even her shrewd child explorer knows the importance of learning from your years. Like the Melville of *Billy Budd*, she realizes that adult innocence is not only oxymoronic but a liability as well. These tumbling stanzas and falling conjunctions compose neither a life nor a poem. Despite the first-person presence, the poem seems distant, willed, and ignorant. Unlike the patriarchal addenda to Gregorio's life, the family affairs cited here inspire little appreciation of this house as a home. If Bishop had visualized this home from without (remembering her stated purpose to depict a Cuban house in Key West), detailing the unsearchable, she might have made a more genuine poem. The attempt, however, to appropriate and even colonize social habitat and cultural habits from which she feels alienated nullifies itself.

If Bishop suffers mixed successes with these writings on home and family, she finds servant and master situations equally troubling. "Faustina, or Rock Roses," "Cootchie," "Manuelzinho," and "Squatter's Children" demand reconsideration of these problems of voice and knowledge from the vantage of the displaced observer. This elected displacement situates Bishop in a most congenial role, that of (as Pound would have James) "true recorder." Yet even this posture requires accommodation to these foreign settings.

Letters to Robert Lowell suggest that Bishop wavered between another first-person reportage and the favored, proven eye of the observer in "Faustina" [CS]. Faustina's situation and language trouble Bishop. The subject seems an unlikely historian of her own situation:

> She [Faustina] speaks a sort of elementary gibberish of her own, part Spanish, part English. [November 18, 1947]

> It is hard to choose among the various versions she gives of her life. [December 3, 1947]

Because Faustina's lack of an adequate means of expression compels the observer to re-invent her history and impose a suitable language, Bishop, with a surgical precision comparable to Stevens's "The Emperor of Ice-Cream," invokes the distorted clutter of a "crazy house" to speak to and of the life of both servant and mistress. Rather than simply portraying a foreign life or unfamiliar circumstances, these musings stand at the center of Bishop's concern with discovering an adequate language of mortality. The power of this language accounts for the relative success of the poem.

Bishop reveals the shifting relative circumstances — the ending of servitude, the waning of life — of Faustina and her mistress through a shift into formlessness and colorlessness, or polarization of colors, which will eventually attempt to resolve itself in simple black and white. Faustina will be the survivor as she quite literally rises above the decay and misery of both mistress and dwelling. Bishop indulges in no grotesquerie here; she offers a factual, though highly selective, rendering of a scene she actually witnessed. As the "visitor" here, she "sits and watches," not expecting the sudden involvement that the situation foists upon her. Within this rather arch, artificial and dying family, Bishop finds herself at home.

"Faustina" consists of two levels of involvement: the interior scene and the exterior characters. A comparable constricting atmosphere occurs in Stevens's "Emperor": When the poem draws its gaze from the funeral meats, it inventories the death-bed scene:

> Take from the dresser of deal,
> Lacking the three glass knobs, that sheet
> On which she embroidered fantails once
> And spread it so as to cover her face.
> If her horny feet protrude, they come
> To show how cold she is, and dumb.
> Let the lamp affix its beam.
> The only emperor is the emperor of ice-cream.

The familiar environment collapses into and around the deceased; life's projects sour in the presence of death. As in "Faustina," death permeates the mistress's "effects," and the objects not only represent but seem to suffer the fate of their owner.

The mistress of Faustina, confined to a perverse life-in-death atmosphere, dwells

> in a crazy house
> upon a crazy bed,
> frail, of chipped enamel,
> blooming above her head
> into four vaguely roselike
> flower-formations . . .

[CP, 72]

The domestic scene is in perceptual and literal disarray. Sagging floorboards, a crooked table, and boxes of "half-crystallized" pills represent the impending deaths of the house, the inhabitants, and a way of life already thoroughly outdated. Even the natural embellishments—a pair of glow-worms—become part of the entropic atmosphere. In a rather anti-Marvellian, antipastoral gesture, these glow-worms illuminate the death chamber with their insistent coloring:

> The visitor sits and watches
> the dew glint on the screen
> and in it two glow-worms
> burning a drowned green.

In this macabre scene of "drowned green," of nature consumed by art, the spectral and the spectatorly fuse the grim with the comic observation.

The fan "she holds but cannot wield" lies useless; the "disordered sheets" sprawl like wilted roses. Finally the material stuff of life tumbles into

> Clutter of trophies,
> chamber of bleached flags!
> —Rags or ragged garments
> hung on the chairs and hooks
> each contributing its
> shade of white, confusing
> as undazzling.

The inanimate thrives only through utility. As the mistress begins to turn from life, her very possessions lose their useful form and momentarily assume the sad grandeur of ceremonial objects. In Bishop's ironic rendering, ordinary domestic possessions literally become "shade[s]," as well as assuming a single, absorptive shade.

The "trophies," "bleached flags," and "Rags or ragged garments" embody the disparity between tropes of life and tropes of death, which invariably contain each other. The monochromatic uniformity that absorbs the individuality and character of the mistress and her material goods, like a blank page, warns that at this premature moment no one can tell whether a temporary victory or immediate surrender to immateriality looms ahead. This choral question, however, will be reconsidered at the closure.

Faustina herself proffers the material of surrender. The mistress, bedridden (requiring soothing talcum) and malfunctioning (nourished solely on the smooth and bland foods of the dying), is no match for the astringent Faustina who "request[s] for herself / a little *cognac*." In matters of posture and sustenance and attitude, Faustina has triumphed over her mistress; she survives. How insidious the verbal exchange between them becomes when viewed in this light: "By and by the whisper / says, '*Faustina, Faustina* . . .' / '¡*Vengo, señora!*'" Bishop's orchestration of witness ("visitor"), victim (employer-mistress), and survivor (Faustina) reveals how she makes this theatrical *exteriority* reach for sympathy—the entire emotional scene lit by an 80-watt bulb.

In title, introduction, and posture, Faustina seems to be suffering a reversal in her life. From the outset the poem suggests that the changes suffered within are beneficial, but there is a sinister current of upheaval and change. The crazy house existence recalls the Poundian world of "Visits to Saint Elizabeths." Bishop acknowledges a Brechtian reversal of roles, but in so doing suggests something frightening and true about the difficulty of comprehending this alien situation of mistress and servant. Each character must be self-contained, a self-auditor, as the commonality of the situation demands. Were it not for that betraying bulb illuminating and isolating "the concern / within our stupefaction," there would be no human intersections in this scene; the "white woman" would be whispering to herself, Faustina "complaining" and "explaining," the visitor sitting and watching. How fatally effective the possessive pronoun *our* seems in the progression of the poem. Tropes of decline stage the argument; the illumination of fully matured imagery "exposes the fine white hair, / the gown with the undershirt / showing at the neck." Indeed, this beam is as merciless as Stevens's surgical light in "The Emperor of Ice-Cream." The poem teeters between what was and what might be. The fear of that uncertainty claims the sympathy of everyone but Faustina. She stands as perhaps the only individual to triumph, and as such takes on the callous, vengeful, and triumphant stance of Brecht's Pirate Jenny.

Bishop expresses her sense of place in a series of tropes of class awareness. Indifferent to the cultural and locutionary distinctions that separate spectator from participant (and servant from mistress), she dwells on the excruciating isolation of class. She seeks neither political caricature nor sentimental bonding with the oppressed, but puzzles over the difficulty of finding a language in which to order this historical situation, which includes the issue of Faustina's survival:

> On bare scraping feet
> Faustina nears the bed.
> ....
> She bends above the other.
> Her sinister kind face
> presents a cruel black
> coincident conundrum.

In Faustina's strangeness lies the threatening mystery. Our ignorance can only lead to the interpretive extremes of "time and silence," "protection and rest"—or the "unimaginable nightmare / that never before dared last / more than a second."

The inability to pierce the successive layers of our ignorance of class, race, language, and history heightens the vaguely sinister and hostile closure. The acuteness of the interpretive questions "starts / a snake-tongue flickering." Unable to rely on language, the visitor turns to the eyes for a clue or response; but finally she can offer only "her bunch / of rust-perforated roses / and wonder oh, whence come / all the petals." This final gesture, warding off other concerns, links visitor with the plight of the mistress. The sickroom roses become the adornment of the sickbed itself.

The haunting depiction of this approximate family (or rather dependency) relationship draws life from its remove. Skirting the casual, interior issues, Bishop views this as one more populated scene. She allows the "things" of life to speak for themselves, and finds in the articles testimony to our relative conditions. A different "family" arrangement forms the Brazilian familial context of "Manuelzinho" [QT]. As if to excuse the amused distance and tone of this first-person account, Bishop attributes the voice to a "friend of the writer," but the situation requires more information than this. Part of what troubles these provincial writings is the language barrier. If Bishop's friend is Brazilian (Bishop declares in correspondence that the speaker is, in fact, Lota de Macedo Soares), then the poem might reasonably make greater allowance for cultural differences between speaker and subject, and deal more naturalistically with the obvious class differences. If the friend is a fellow-foreigner, why not simply have Bishop tell the tale? The autobiographical first-person voice is problematic in most of Bishop's poems, but here the account seems a step too removed, insulating reader and author alike from the social and emotional core of the dramatic situation.

By avoiding the abrupt reversals of "Faustina," which map the emotionally hierarchical drama that poem enacts, "Manuelzinho" offers a gentle though condescending and psychologically evasive portrait of the landed speaker and the peasant-subject. The account of this relationship explores this notion of landed ownership, inheritance, and rights, and acknowledges with exasperation the landowner's obligation toward the poor. The poem begins by unfolding its dominant trope of hierarchy:

> Half squatter, half tenant (no rent) —
> a sort of inheritance; white,
> in your thirties now, and supposed
> to supply me with vegetables,
> but you don't; or you won't; or you can't
> get the idea through your brain —
> the world's worst gardener since Cain.

> [CP, 96]

The voice of this poem not only suggests its own class superiority to Manuelzinho, but implicitly condemns both his situation and his character. Through obstinacy, ignorance, or innocence he has failed to live up to his obligations to his superior. *Supposed* carries the charge that *ought* might when used similarly. The words of the superior betray a mild irritation, but her tone suggests worse possibilities. Abusing class privilege, she assumes a godly, judicial power over this uncerebral criminal, associating him, with sweeping inappropriateness, with the famous murderer whose punishment was his lack of success at gardening.

If not actually guilty, Manuelzinho does seem accursed. He is plagued by incidents uncommon to others: misshapen produce, floods, and "umbrella ants." In the isolation of his fate, Manuelzinho takes possession (in almost tribal fashion) of the land. The speaker oscillates between amusement and discomfort as she considers the tandem ownership:

> I watch you through the rain,
> trotting, light, on bare feet,
> up the steep paths you have made —
> or your father and grandfather made —
> all over my property,
> with your head and back inside
> a sodden burlap bag,
> and feel I can't endure it
> another minute; then,
> indoors, beside the stove,
> keep on reading a book.

This lithe nimbleness appears again in Crusoe's companion, Friday. The speaker knows true ownership when she sees it. Not only does the land belong to Manuelzinho through ancestry, but also through nature: He knows the land. In him occurs a struggle among spirit, nature, and intellect, but he is unable to voice that struggle, and can only reveal it through his uncertainty, unreliability, ineptitude, and occasional surprising grace.

As the curious coincidences and occurrences double up, they begin to define a rhetorical and emotional distancing. Not only is Bishop, the omniscient shaper of this poem, quarreling with both foreigners, but she is attempting to align the knowledge of the gardener with that of the artist, much as criminal and saint are already mutually implicated. As Manuelzinho carries the blame for both the miraculous and the criminal, he seems less isolated and dependent in his difference. By embracing all of the roles available to the impoverished, Manuelzinho begins to assume an almost human form; however, because all of these roles perish in the blast of the speaker's disdain he has to seek his identity in the other world:

> And once I yelled at you
> so loud to hurry up
> and fetch me those potatoes
> your holey hat flew off,
> you jumped out of your clogs,
> leaving three objects arranged
> in a triangle at my feet,
> as if you'd been a gardener
> in a fairy tale all this time
> and at the word "potatoes"
> had vanished to take up your work
> of fairy prince somewhere.

Reduced to curlike status in this hierarchical world of "fetch" and "jump," Manuelzinho still manages to invoke a magical transport to "somewhere." Reminiscent of the "Elsewhere" designation of one section of *Questions of Travel*, the gardener's "somewhere" categorizes an "other" world where Manuelzinho, out of sight of his employer, lives a more authentic life. Denying Manuelzinho the agency of "art" (though he is artistlike, it is his *absence* that makes the art) frees the poet to discover the design ("leaving three objects arranged / in a triangle at [the speaker's] feet" [cf. the "bird's art" in "Sunday, 4 A.M.") underlying their relationship, which mingles religious and fairytale motifs and avoids the psychological complexities of an encounter between two adults.

Rather than admit to being in the presence of a potential artist, savior, or criminal (who at least attains self-sufficiency), the speaker patronizes Manuelzinho as a kind of half-grown child. She absorbs him in a mock-familial arrangement that will care for the gardener through sickness and heath, wealth and poverty. She refuses to admit she detects Manuelzinho's spirit, though it compels her to describe him in biblical and saintly terms, and chooses instead to characterize him as a mindless if congenial helper. In her uncertainty as to whether he is saint, criminal, or fool she wavers:

> In the kitchen we dream together
> how the meek shall inherit the earth —
> or several acres of mine.

Unable to retain the image of Manuelzinho as a version of St. Francis, however, she settles for the alternate view of him as a chiseling halfwit.

A foggy mist similar to the one that yielded to reveal Balthazár in "Twelfth Morning" shrouds Manuelzinho as he drifts with his Biblical jackass, standing fixed in place morning and evening as if allowing sufficient time to absorb the magnificence and significance of the scene before him. As if to excuse her lack of interpretive clarity, the speaker attributes her visual confusion to "a few / big, soft, pale-blue, / sluggish fireflies, / the jellyfish of the air" that have fallen between them, muddling the picture. Thus relieved of any obligation to see Manuelzinho as he really is, the speaker retreats into a world in which her own limitations are natural law.

The poem allows only a glimpse of that "other" family, Manuelzinho's own. Children scuttle about like lower forms of life, typified as "little moles aboveground." The wife performs only the role of the seamstress who keeps her husband patched. These dependents and subordinate caretakers are allowed little space in the larger tale. The gardener's well-being rests in the hands of the feudal landowner-narrator, not of his wife and children.

The coda rejects the sophisticated, public slander to which the mistress subjects her gardener, in front of guests. The poem does not say whether Manuelzinho was humiliated by his cruel nickname, "Klorophyll Kid" (inspired by the bright green brim he painted on his hat), or whether he even understood, but his mistress knew how unkind it was. As she reacts to this secret cruelty, she recognizes something characteristic in herself in the pleasure she finds in using her friend for a joke, drawing attention to the class and economic tension between them. Bishop seems to suggest that although such situations require humanity, they usually settle for mere civility:

> . . . Unkindly,
> I called you Klorophyll Kid.
> My visitors thought it was funny.
> I apologize here and now.
>
> You helpless, foolish man,
> I love you all I can,
> I think. Or do I?
> I take off my hat, unpainted
> and figurative, to you.
> Again I promise to try.

The uncertainties in this closure typify Bishop's unease with both the voice of this poem and the two portraits it generates, the one of Manuelzinho and the one of the speaker. The poem leaves residual misunderstandings and important issues unresolved. The question remains: What has been learned? Can one extend love to an alien, a stranger, an outcast? Can the rich landowner find humanity in a grown man she can only perceive as "helpless, foolish"? What kind of moral demonstration is it that offers only a visual, figurative gesture to this most literal of men? Apologies and promises cannot penetrate the strangeness of the man and his ways. Manuelzinho, distinct from the speaker in class, economic status, world-view, and his baffling criminal saintliness, remains enigmatic to her.

Unlike the Wordsworthian solitaries or the Emersonian "country people . . . [who] sympathize with every log & foreknow its every nod & stir with chain & crowbar & seem to see through the ground all the accidents of preservation & decay" (transformed by the intellect and language of the poets), Bishop's provincials carry with them their transient tongues. Thus the poet attempts to capture the "transient" oral voice with the "deliberate" voice of a culture that prizes a high degree of literacy. The difficulty of catching oral intonations and fixing them on the page have defeated most modern poets, Robert Frost most obviously excepted. In her poems in *North & South* drawn from the black American subculture, Bishop fully exposes her lack of a comprehending ear for culturally derived language distinctions, especially those still energized by oral rhythms and wordplay. Despite her benign intentions, she generates in "Songs for a Colored Singer" the artificial rhetoric of Gosden and Correll as Amos and Andy, while a more sophisticated level of diction sputters and fails her in the meditative piece "Cootchie." Unprepared to generate a stunning portrait like "Faustina," Bishop fumbles shyly for the tone and voice of true appreciation and tribute, but is foiled by her distrust of such conventional modes of discourse.

In "Cootchie," the first of these attempts, Bishop reaches for a sincere register of loss. As she wrote to Moore on February 29, 1940:

> I am enclosing another one that may be banal. I can't decide. Maybe you will remember Cootchie — I don't know what Miss Lula is going to do without her, she had lived with her thirty-five years.

The fear of the ordinariness of this elegy fails to suggest the troubling nature of the diction in this poem. The very name *Cootchie* repels the gentleness of the elegy, refusing its comfort. Unlike Eudora Welty or Flannery O'Connor, natives to the sounds and customs of the South, Bishop here seems as deaf as Miss Lula. Instead of marking this death in a dignified manner, this poem is artfully but jocose and contrived, offkey, and somewhat offhand. However valued Cootchie was, she cannot—as Bishop well knows—sustain the mock-Miltonic weight of

> Searching the land and sea for someone else,
> the lighthouse will discover Cootchie's grave
> and dismiss all as trivial; the sea, desperate,
>   will proffer wave after wave.

[CP, 46]

A strong elegy requires more of an edge, a commanding tone, or a heightened, revealing incident like the terminal exchange in "Faustina" to embody either a life or the poignancy of its passing.

The disturbing and untrustworthy voice, the result of mistaking conventional racist parody for the actuality of African-American speech, turns each of these poems into something other than an Elizabeth Bishop poem. In the discomfiting sequence "Songs for a Colored Singer," her four-part tribute to Billie Holiday, a gradually modulating voice surfaces from the counterfeit idiom of Parts I and II promising, but not accomplishing, the genuine pitch of Bishop's voice. Though Bishop calls these pieces "songs," their rhythmic qualities fail to sustain effective lyricism. She avoids the most painful kind of dialect, but slips into vaudeville idioms that are equally distressing. She sounds like an amateur thespian drifting from the broadest parody of singer and Le Roy to the voice of a somewhat abashed white poet:

> I say, "Le Roy, just how much are we owing?
> Something I can't comprehend,
> the more we got the more we spend. . . ."
> He only answers, "Let's get going."
> Le Roy, you're earning too much money now.

[CP, 47]

Not only is it difficult to imagine Bishop writing these lines, but they do not sound as if they could ever be spoken by anyone. Is it credible that this "colored singer" would reach out with that ironic "he sure has an inquiring mind?" Though Bishop's own voice struggles to surface, the unconvincing "blackface" persona triumphs. (For example, compare the ironically autobiographical blackface voice in Berryman's *The Dream Songs*.) Bishop's best poetry rests on the "knowledge of the traveler," but these songs, written by a poet who never psychologically braved the ghetto, sound like cribbings from an imperfectly heard Holiday recording.

Though the lyric choral interjection in "Song II" ("The time has come to call a halt") provides momentary relief from the obnoxious blackface tone, the poem still fails to either invent a convincing dialect voice or allow Bishop's own voice to emerge. It is difficult not to wince at the jarring mimicry of

> I met him walking with Varella
> and hit him twice with my umbrella.

or

> Far down the highway wet and black
> I'll ride and ride and not come back.
> I'm going to go and take the bus
> and find someone monogamous.

since the speech imitated here has never existed. How differently Bishop has handled exile, hurt, and poverty elsewhere, when she has not felt compelled to appropriate a voice of such meager scope and diction. For her to be successful, she must place her intelligence in control; her voice, with all its elegance and euphony, must be the voice of the poem. The closing stanzas of "Going to the Bakery" [CP1, 206] a later poem (1968), provide such an example:

> In front of my apartment house
> a black man sits in a black shade,
> lifting his shirt to show a bandage
> on his black, invisible side.
>
> Fumes of *cachaça* knock me over,
> like gas fumes from an auto-crash.

> He speaks in perfect gibberish.
> The bandage glares up, white and fresh.
>
> I give him seven cents in *my*
> terrific money, say "Good night"
> from force of habit. Oh, mean habit!
> Not one word more apt or bright?
>
> [CP, 152]

The words that matter are Bishop's own. Her appropriation of this man's anguish and fear by imposing a language more domesticated than his own, while not entirely convincing, deprives him of what should be his most important possession.

Part III of "Songs," taking a cue from the refrain of Part II ("The time has come . . ."), seeks refuge in a lullaby that seems related to "Cootchie":

> Lullaby.
> Adult and child
> sink to their rest.
> At sea the big ship sinks and dies,
> lead in its breast.
>
> [CP, 49]

Tapping the universal scope of "Cootchie," Bishop attempts to scale the sorrow of this singer's life, her prisonlike existence:

> Let nations rage,
> let nations fall.
> The shadow of the crib makes an enormous cage
> upon the wall.

These songs, individually and as a group, fail to generate sufficient emotional expectations. By itself this song is silent, but clearly requires a context. It is uncertain whether this is a *cri de coeur* or a guilty social conscience.

In the final song, Bishop approaches but can only partly engage her own voice. Here she responds to the commonality, not the peculiar individuality, of the singer's life. In the midst of echoes of earlier songs, however, resounds the richer, still undeveloped voice of "Sestina":

What's that shining in the leaves,
the shadowy leaves,
like tears when somebody grieves,
shining, shining in the leaves?

[CP, 50]

The conflation of rain and the tears that carry knowledge will occur again when the almanac advises "Time to plant tears." Even if Bishop later felt that this final song was merely an excuse to approximate a Billie Holiday song, she at least had sounded a more authentic voice with which to close.

Faced with the intriguing strangeness of Key West, Brazil, and even black America, Bishop could not make her available language and socialization entirely coincide with the immediate resources of the culture. She attempted to push the tradition of provincial lyric poetry beyond her native culture and knowledge, rejecting the comfortable language of the picturesque, and ran the attendant risks. Early works like "Faustina" and "Gregorio Valdes" show an instinctive rightness of tone and stance, largely in the adroit use of settings and description, that Bishop would later recover and develop. Comparing "At the Fishhouses" with Wordsworth's "Resolution and Independence" or "Michael," or with Yeats's "The Fisherman" demonstrates Bishop's consummate skill with familiar material; while comparing such fully realized works with even her best Brazil poems illustrates her unease with situations in which landscape, character, and language do not, for her, fully cohere.

CHAPTER 6

Crusoe at Home

Examining Bishop's various attempts to generate a sufficient and viable language for her poetry raises the question of whether Bishop always required single perspectives (that of the child or provincial, for instance) or whether she wrote poems that attained a coherent, inclusive model of her universe. Is there a poem in the canon that embodies the entire complexity of her experience and vision? Do any of her poems achieve a language powerful and variable enough to reconcile a whole world of regrets and compensations, one that resolves the dichotomies of exterior and interior experience, perception and desire? Can any language adequately conform to experience? Though many of these issues have been addressed in individual poems, the work before *Geography III* recognizes but does not integrate the mutual otherness of self and situation. Indeed, in spite of the presence of "old correspondences," metaphors of unity and integration, most of Bishop's poems before *Geography III* resist imposing order on "the untidy activity [that] continues, / awful but cheerful." Bishop requires a language and rhetoric more (or less) inclusive, flexible, earthy, and homey than the romantic sublime, the epiphany, or the picturesque to explore the concerns of her maturity; she has reached a point in her life and writing that demands awareness of the whole. Discrete particulars will not do; her task requires utter coherence.

Bishop's recollections of a trip to Aruba ("it's true that there are small volcanoes all over the place") and rediscovering "how really awful Robinson Crusoe was" prompted what many feel to be her finest poem, "Crusoe in England" (1971). The immediate critical reception of the book was quite laudatory. Helen Vendler believed that "A poet who has written this poem really needs to write nothing else: it seems . . . a perfect reproduction of the self in words"; David Kalstone saw Bishop involved with "the questions *after* travel, a kind of 'Dejection Ode' countered by the force and energy that memory has mustered for the rest of the poem" and that the *Geography III* poems are "more openly inner landscapes than ever before." The confiding tone of this fictional reminiscence, the achievement of a comprehensive language of self-invention, the deceptive self-sufficiency of art and the final inadequacy of the self-created world, are the concerns of this chapter. In the course of this dramatic monologue, Bishop disrupts generic expectations and traditions, reveals the child's vision behind the weary recollections of an agéd exile, and locates the human bond in the very inadequacy of language. The voice of this poem argues that all knowledge, finally, is incomplete, and consists not of ends but of paths, processes, maps, ways. "Crusoe in England" provides the threshold to "One Art," an elegy for Bishop's attempt to grasp and possess her world through poetic achievement.

Adopting the voice of a male exile and refusing the privileges of autobiography, risking the glaze of distance Lowell noted in Browning's monologues, Bishop paradoxically heightens the immediacy of her "Crusoe" with a weary tonality of such authenticity her character seems not an extension of Defoe's fictional exile but a real Crusoe, endowed with a twentieth-century emotional frankness. The monologue seems the ideal form to tell the story of a prototype of Melville's *isolatoes*, since it enables Bishop to provide a maplike form of a life without adhering to disruptive chronology. The meanderings of the individual mind, a twentieth-century idea of a literary model, lends a degree of authenticity that owes more to Joyce and Freud than to Defoe or Melville. "Crusoe" assumes the appearance without running the risks of an autobiography by ordering its experience into what Robert Lowell in an interview describes as "a shape that answers better than mere continuous experience."

Though the progenitive tale (Defoe's *The Life and Adventures of Robinson Crusoe* [1719]) posits a Christian context for the exile (and in some respects retains a Miltonic world-view for its sense of education and redemption), "Crusoe in England" discards all dogma while retaining the skeleton of the saintly and prophetic wilderness-quest. Bishop's poem might be considered an "education of the exile" poem, but it does not equate the return to civilization with salvation. Crusoe, after all, was exiled into, not out of, paradise. Unlike its fictional counterpart, the poem tells us nothing about this Crusoe's prior life — except that it began in England. The emotional intensity, viewed retrospectively, of the relationship with Friday indicates the most important respect in which the Bishop poem extends Defoe's character. In many ways, most of Bishop's poetry offers the viewpoint of an outsider: she is in turn the child at knee level, the language-deprived traveler, or, less convincingly, the provincial. Early ("Man-Moth") and late ("Pink Dog") examples of her personae of exile illustrate her fascination with extreme isolation, with freaks and outcasts. Though their admittedly distorted perspectives are convincing, they engender no sense of kinship, nor are they intended to. Their purpose is to engender languages of extremity, and to plot with their grotesque narratives the border beyond which the psyche and language no longer appear to coincide.

Robert Lowell has most clearly described the kind of difference found in Bishop's exile poems. When discussing the uniqueness of "The Man-Moth" [NS] he said:

> In Elizabeth Bishop's "Man-Moth" a whole new world is gotten out and you don't know what will come after any one line. It's exploring. And it's as original as Kafka. She's gotten a world, not just a way of writing. She seldom writes a poem that doesn't have the exploring quality.

The otherworldliness of "The Man-Moth" beckons; like the shadows of German Expressionist films, it looms uncomfortably near enough to darken the familiar world. The man-moth is an oddly plausible figure, drawn to the surface from tunnels and nightmares of the ordinary imagination. The "whole new world" he occupies depends upon negatives or opposites: shadow and light, verticals and horizontals, forward and backward, sun and moon. The shadowy mirror-images (unlike the playful distortions of "The Gentleman of Shalott") challenge his grip on the surface of the earth just as they challenge the ordinary viewer to define a comfortable self-image, a grip on sanity.

Yet even this world of negatives and opposites has limits and rules. The Man-Moth's discomfort during this "visit to the surface" is palpable. The nature of his other life, underground, remains undetermined; but unlike Crusoe this alien shares, somewhat unwillingly, what humanity he contains:

> If you catch him,
> hold up a flashlight to his eye. It's all dark pupil,
> an entire night itself, whose haired horizon tightens
> as he stares back, and closes up the eye. Then from the lids
> one tear, his only possession, like the bee's sting, slips.
> Slyly he palms it, and if you're not paying attention
> he'll swallow it. However, if you watch, he'll hand it over,
> cool as from underground springs and pure enough to drink.
>
> [CP, 15]

The Man-Moth's humanity reveals itself only in the terms of its subterranean world, the "entire night" of its eye, its single tear.

Bishop conjures similarly self-inhibited spirits throughout her writing. For example, in "Gwendolyn" part of the child's self-definition required definition of her opposites, in somewhat the way the adult process of self-discovery might entail an encounter with an opposite in the form of a Man-Moth–like creature. Bishop's larger concern is to generate a language of sufficient latitude to permit observation of these intersections of like and unlike. The actions of Crusoe occur within a carefully depicted emotional frame, but the Man-Moth embodies the unknown or the unconscious, "an entire night in itself." In the end, his surfacing is an incomplete gesture, an attempt to reach out to others that is partially negated by his unwillingness to make a gift of his emotional self. The truncated first lines of these stanzas indicate how very tentative this gesture really is. Though the images are tethered to the knowable world, the poem heightens the contrast between shadow and light, the strangeness of ordinary landscapes, and the potential oddities of perspective. Bishop has dramatized the way the ordinary daylight world forcibly persuades the outsider to conform:

he climbs fearfully, thinking that this time he will manage
to push his small head through that round clean opening
and be forced through, as from a tube, in black scrolls on the
    light.

The rather grim simile — "as from a tube" — underscores the solitary
nature of his journey; society has no place for him, no means of
accommodating such a creature. The compactness of his world,
the tension of his stance, in these lines is oppressive. The density of
the stanzas, the longish lines dominated by monosyllables, suggest
what the Man-Moth must penetrate. These contrasting worlds of
shadow and light, underground and surface seem mutually exclu-
sive, beyond interpretation or knowledge. The ordinary world has
broken down into cubist planes of darkness and reflected light,
while the poet-observer stands to one side, manipulating those reflections in the terms of self-definition.

Unlike this misprint hero, however, some of Bishop's exiles fail
to contrive even an alternate life. Edwin Boomer in the story "The
Sea and Its Shore" cannot grasp the missing interpretive links in
his world of literary litter; he lacks the societal awareness necessary
to find meaning in such debris. Boomer's lantern reappears in "The
Prodigal," but this time offers no light: "The lantern — like the sun,
going away — / laid on the mud a pacing aureole." Illumination
lies adjacent to, but forever out of reach of, this liquor-sodden
outcast; only spirits, not his own, infuse him with courage to en-
dure "his exile yet another year or more." "The Burglar of Baby-
lon" fails to win sympathy because of a lack of antecedent material
(perhaps the folk ballad form itself subverts the poem's intensity
by subjecting the psychological tension to overly linear narrative
strategies). The poem generates neither sympathy nor guilt; the
central figure remains too distanced for pity or even the enlighten-
ment of the reader. The only possible interface between so unem-
pathic an exile and his unintegrated world is a violent one, a colli-
sion of sorts.

"Pink Dog," a late poem of exile, offers the opportunity to appreciate the depth, breadth, and humanity of the works that lead
to "Crusoe in England." Perhaps Bishop said all she had to say in
"Crusoe," for it is difficult not to turn her observation — "awful
but cheerful" — against this late exercise in irony and scorn. To

appreciate the unusual qualities of this poem, however, is to instinctively know the rightness of "Crusoe."

While refusing the predictable moral stance, "Pink Dog" exposes the cruelties of an age of extreme conformity. The poem, however, lacks Bishop's characteristic vaguely resigned but painfully aware voice, and affects a tone of humorous indifference. Though she may attempt to echo the less-than-acute political satire of the Brazilian sambas (see translation in CP 263–264) and simultaneously record the trials of the dog and the brutalized narrator, she relies on a series of tropes of the grotesque that engender neither nor interest. Surely she would recognize that the speaker of this poem is as much a victim of a cruel age as the dog. Lacking the sting of political narrative, Bishop's critique appears naïve, not shrewd. The light-verse end rhymes of the tercets of "Pink Dog," rather than intensifying and unifying the poem, render it comical and tasteless. Perhaps a difficulty with this poem stems from its strange voice. Though the voice of "Manuelzinho" was not Bishop's, the attendant spirit's voice was. "Pink Dog" lacks the strong sense of purpose found in even the weaker of the earlier exile pieces. As so often, Randall Jarrell most effectively describes what most have come to expect from Bishop's world, and in so doing reveals the sullied vision of this poem:

> She is so morally attractive in poems like "The Fish" or "Roosters" because she understands so well that the wickedness and confusion of the age can explain and extenuate other people's wickedness and confusion, but not for you, your own; that morality, for the individual, is usually a small, personal, statistical, but heartbreaking or heartwarming affair of omissions and commissions the greatest of which will seem infinitesimal, ludicrously beneath notice, to those who govern, rationalize, and deplore.

The lack of that moral attractiveness mars "Pink Dog," but the poem does remind the reader how convincingly that moral purpose occurs in her best work, like "Crusoe."

Commentators have made much of the strangeness of the landscape of Crusoe's island; it echoes Melville's Encantadas, Darwin's descriptions of the Galápagos Islands, and Bishop's own vacation notes of a trip to Aruba. Developing the rich traditions of travel literature and playing against those garden poems that place a green shade against a contaminated world, Bishop extends a distinct tradition in the terms of the American pastoral.

From Natty and Chingachgook to Huck and Jim, and Ishmael and Queequeg, American couples have found adventure and purpose in the wilderness. Crusoe, like his literary ancestors and descendants, leaves the green shade of England, suffers a period of trial and uncertainty, but finds *life* in that incomprehensible world of that other island. The American pastoral illustrates the impossibility of lingering in the primitive world; the imperatives of human intelligence forbid it. In Crusoe's narrative, however, exterior forces, not his or Friday's intelligence or will, foster the return to civilized values. They perish, as a couple in mutual exile, when they are saved (Friday in fact literally dies of civilization in the form of measles). If Bishop intended to invoke the garden genre when she placed Crusoe once again on the barren volcanic island, she did so to emphasize the growth of Crusoe himself. Only one kind of creature flourishes when planted there, the human kind. Rather than functioning as a garden of humanity, however, a site of the creation myth, the island bears the impress of only one other individual, Friday, whose sex fails to complement Crusoe's.

From the opening stanza, Bishop is concerned not merely with the boundaries of communication — accounts, registers, books, poems, names, sayings, reading — but with the dependence of all these on social interaction, a human context. What meaning can a name have when there is no one with whom to share its significance? Books previously read show no signs of assisting Crusoe in this island world: "The books / I'd read were full of blanks." All degrees of order seem suspect: Crusoe finds joy and music in his homemade flute in spite of its weird scale, but he relinquishes his hold on language; words belong elsewhere.

The cacophony of *baa*, *shriek*, *hiss* reiterates the unimportance of embellished utterance. On this island, necessity dictates: The gut speaks. Yet Crusoe yearns for reciprocity. His insularity prompts a malignant introversion; dreams play off his daylight fears. Soon he understands his solitary state in the human enterprise as not merely a term of exile, but forever.

The ultimate erasure of language occurs at the moment of intimate resolution of the state of exile:

> Just when I thought I couldn't stand it
> another minute longer, Friday came.
> (Accounts of that have everything all wrong.)
>
> [CP, 165]

After the nightmarish threat of intellectual pedantry throughout eternity, Crusoe surrenders his civilization. His need for contact with his own kind confounds his emotional grasp of the state of exile. Ordinary language, the language of accounts, cannot grasp the utter disruption of Crusoe's established emotional state triggered by the direct physical confrontation with a healthy otherness; in retrospect, unable to conjure a more emotive language, Crusoe can only confess that

> Friday was nice.
> Friday was nice, and we were friends.

Yet the effect of this apparent failure of rhetorical prowess is to reiterate the original emotional value of these simple words. If language preserved itself for occasions of significance (as this encounter suggests), the apparent numbness of the cliché dissipates. With casual, offhand language, Bishop deliberately cloaks the interiority of this relationship. Unlike Defoe, who immediately establishes Crusoe and Friday as a hierarchical master–servant relationship, Bishop fosters the immediate equality of friendship. She has chosen to approximate the "infant sight" of original relationship with these deliberately disposable words, but in doing so she raises the issue of dramatic plausibility. Can it be that the Crusoe who is so able to recount and register his world and experiences alone is unable to articulate beyond these vague utterances the details of his saving relationship with Friday? Or is the subtle linguistic argument intended to be his own?

Judging the appropriateness of Crusoe's superficial recall requires examining the coda with some care. In examining his life in terms of the physical artifacts, one of the questions Crusoe must resolve is whether his narrative is the stuff of poetry. The problem seems less one of an inability to express (surely Bishop does not intend these items to serve as objective correlatives) than one pertaining to a sense of decorum. A stern aesthetic forbids the inclusion of tropes of sentimentality or, worse, formless abstraction. An effective narrative must derive its power from Bishop's ability to indicate the absence of sentiment and analysis and allow unspoken and aesthetically unspeakable language to reveal itself under erasure, taking form from the reader's, rather than Crusoe's or Bishop's, experience of mind and soul. Surely this degree of verbal intimacy is the keenest possible between the reader and poet.

Like Stevens's "The Man on the Dump," Crusoe's task is to invent a language, however primal or trite, of self-definition. As he beats on his lard pail on his island dump, he sounds the idioms of exhaustion, a language of despair. The world consists of debris, the island a "cloud-dump" with "left-over clouds." Even the water becomes dusty and vaguely landlike as the watersprouts are "scuffed-up white." The one tree, "a sooty-scrub affair," tropes on the futility of attempting to inhabit this burned-over district; credible living occurs elsewhere. In spite of the episodes of home crafts and simple pleasures,

> There was one kind of berry, a dark red.
> I tried it, one by one, and hours apart.
> Sub-acid and not bad, no ill effects;
> and so I made home-brew. I'd drink
> the awful, fizzy, stinging stuff
> that went straight to my head
> and play my home-made flute
> (I think it had the weirdest scale on earth)
> and, dizzy, whoop and dance among the goats.

The island remains a prehistoric site until Friday comes. Except for this brief respite of human contact and concern, the spirit of this life, as Crusoe recalls it, has "petered out" and "dribbled away." Finally the boredom of the other, home island—England, a real, yet uninteresting world—has corrupted the tongue, which has forgotten how to name the self-sufficiency that must have sustained Crusoe for many years by himself. The closure lacks the predictable and decisive trope of failure, resignation, or self-affirmation. Instead, the rhetoric seems exhausted, and trickles away. From this casual idiom of depletion, which dictates the tone and register of diction of the entire poem, derives the quiet authority of Crusoe's voice.

Framed and punctuated by figurations of experience (the knife-icon, the winemaking, the flute), the internal colloquy assumes a privileged stance, rhetorically empowered by the authority of the central trope of the romance, the quest into the wilderness for knowledge. Surrounded by stanzas devoted to the habitat and to seemingly minor occurrences, the dialogic meditations achieve a fresh radiance, despite their negative tone. Apparently at one time crushed by loneliness, Crusoe reflects on the fragility of the ego and its unease with the naked self:

> I often gave way to self-pity.
> "Do I deserve this? I suppose I must.
> I wouldn't be here otherwise. Was there
> a moment when I actually chose this?
> I don't remember, but there could have been."
> What's wrong about self-pity, anyway?
> With my legs dangling down familiarly
> over a crater's edge, I told myself
> "Pity should begin at home." So the more
> pity I felt, the more I felt at home.

The picture of Crusoe under the "cloud-dump" with his legs dangling "over a crater's edge" mocks the conventional sublimity of Keats's Titans in *Hyperion*. Contemplating the familiar abyss — after the implied self-correction of "What's wrong about self-pity, anyway?" — Crusoe rises above self-absorption, rallying with "Pity should begin at home." The agéd narrator, however, requires a retrospective amendment: "So the more / pity I felt, the more I felt at home." If there is more than a hint of the postlapsarian world in this poem (however genuine the direct observations of the landscapes are), it rests in its godless self-mockery. Bishop allows the preposition *about* to carry the weight of the questioning line, "What's wrong about self-pity, anyway?" Canceling the expected *with*, she turns to its abrupt cousin in the hope of suggesting a problem of view, one surrounded by the dislocations of self-pity. Though Crusoe returns to pity, his crater-colloquy has broadened his horizons.

Melville generates a similarly humane and humorous self-pitying, self-interrogation in the first chapter of *Moby-Dick*. For both Ishmael and Crusoe an unnamable lack of ease triggers inte-

rior, meditative voyages. Ishmael at home, like Crusoe, would die
of boredom, but being at the beginning of his book he still enjoys
the opportunity of an actual if also allegorical voyage. Crusoe has
no such option, and his epic is too brief even to recover the original
journey. The poem offers glimpses but no sustained history; even
those glimpses assume a meditative, lyric concentration, inimical
to narrative flow, when the simple past tense yields occasionally to
the spirited, ever-present participles: "the overlapping rollers / — a
glittering hexagon of rollers / closing and closing in"; the waterspouts "advancing and retreating"; the "hissing, ambulating turtles"; the "spawning," the "knowing," the "registering" of this island existence. The initial voyage and the shipwreck are prehistory.
The world-weary Crusoe suggests through the indirection of selective recall that finally the sustaining aspects of island life were
not the memory of his previous life but the unreal (surreal) and
interesting (unexpected) features of everyday life as an exile. The
relics, in the end, fail to sustain even that limited need to reflect
upon the past:

> The knife there on the shelf —
> it reeked of meaning, like a crucifix.
> It lived. How many years did I
> beg it, implore it, not to break?
> I knew each nick and scratch by heart,
> the bluish blade, the broken tip,
> the lines of wood-grain on the handle . . .
> Now it won't look at me at all.

That need for connections, a gaze returned, also occurs in the
final meditative section of "At the Fishhouses." The recognition
of shared experience through the fetishized artifacts confirms the
historical validity of the reconstructed self. Strange that Bishop
would confer upon the animal and inanimate worlds these powers
of correspondence; but the auditory associations of "Clang!" and
the "scream" of the village, the crazy-quilt and Aunt Mary's doll of
Gwendolyn, the almanac of "Sestina" demonstrate how central the
single isolated notes are to Bishop's recollections. With these she
conjures up entire lifetimes.

"Crusoe in England" retrieves those poems of childhood that
seek to situate the child in her own skin and in society, and antici-

pates (though chronologically succeeding) the landscape poems of the marginal observer of the sea and its shore. Born into the new world naked, a type of the first inhabitant of Bishop's world, Crusoe must first discover his self-identity and then proceed to a relational awareness through his mastery of a sufficient language. With his unsatisfying but undeniable success Crusoe supplies answers to Bishop's seemingly rhetorical questions of travel:

> Think of the long trip home.
> Should we have stayed at home and thought of here?
> Where should we be today?
> Is it right to be watching strangers in a play
> in this strangest of theatres?
> What childishness is it that while there's a breath of life
> in our bodies, we are determined to rush
> to see the sun the other way around?
>
> [CP, 93]

What better way to rediscover one's self through self-education and the schooling of survival? In this island wilderness-garden, lacking community and rejecting history, Crusoe determines and defines home as a viable point of view. In retrospect, he could answer that final question of travel: "Should we have stayed at home, wherever that may be?" The lyric self emerging from the structuring landscape bares a soul linked to this world (this "surrealism of everyday life") while it claims the metaphor of creation and declares itself the finite I AM, only to discover, immediately, that existence is merely one more figure of speech.

As he recalls the new world of his exile, Crusoe lingers lovingly on significant moments of discovery and learning, despair and delight. Like the account of the conquistador tourists of "Brazil, January 1, 1502," this narrative weaves together the languages of metaphysical doubt, discovery, the domestic world, art and artifact, intimacies and geography. It is also an allegory of birth, of entry into the "historical, flowing, and flown." Avoiding the multiple identities of poems like "In the Waiting Room," Crusoe commits himself to no one, not even to his exiled but integrated self. Yet very much like the child's awareness, this moment of relative security purges the tide of self-pity long enough to allow Crusoe to see the world as something other than a self-reflection.

The *memento mori* framing of the poem contains its undelineated history as firmly as the *National Geographic* with its "yellow margins, the date" binds the experience of the waiting room. Between the newspaper account of the volcano's birth and the death of Friday occurs the empowering moment of Crusoe's meditation. These two historical events frame a highly conventionalized world of chronological connections ("Everything connected by 'and' and 'and'"), the calendar and habitat of the quotidian. Unlike Defoe's protagonist (whose moves kept time with England), Crusoe seeks to escape his historical frame and enter another dimension to form an ahistorical life. Told entirely in retrospect, his tale leaves enormous narrative gaps. Crusoe has identified the parentheses of his interior life, and leaves them vacant. He recalls his life as a series of poses vying for attention as the formative or empowering one, a series of moments that erupt, like volcanoes, from the surrounding historical matrix. In recall, chronology yields to lyric and meditative conventions of aporia, indirection, and unexpected juxtaposition.

To see the larger dimensions of Crusoe's self-construction requires a sense of its beginnings. Only knowledge of the "old," "bored" Crusoe of pre-Friday exile can account for the force-field of emotion and experience that follows. By the time of recounting, his life's blood—"that archipelago / has petered out"; the edge of survival "has dribbled away." Even as we see the life materialize, it fades. The reminiscence turned elegy serves primarily to measure the time from Crusoe's release from the island to his figurative death, coincident with Friday's actual one.

To account for himself, Crusoe feels obligated to place his narrative on the terra firma of a particular but peculiar nature. Despite its solid foundation, the scale is disturbing. The puniness of the volcanoes proves unsettling. Deprived of relational certainties, the exile wanders alert yet unknowing. He can judge a place or situation only in relation to the human community, but here there is none. Like Gulliver, Crusoe finds the landscape unsound because disproportioned. Like Alice, he wonders whether he has grown large or the world has grown small. Crusoe would have benefited from a glimpse of those "shadowy gray knees, / trousers and skirts and boots" of the waiting room; at least he could have gauged his size.

The panoramic overview gives way to a another dislocating exercise in scale and perspective. Crusoe sees *his* island in active relation to the sea and sky. Whereas the landscape at first seemed detailed but remote, it now challenges Crusoe's sense of reality. Empiricism fails him. Why the parched craters when it continually rains? Why the constant geologic unease? Why the lack of clear distinction between organic and inorganic forms?

> The folds of lava, running out to sea,
> would hiss. I'd turn. And then they'd prove
> to be more turtles.

Bishop has often returned to the opaque surface of the sea to meditate upon the otherness of the natural world. Always before the ocean has functioned as a restorative trope of otherness; in its difference, its refusal of form, its marbled, restless surfaces, lay its soothing effects. In Crusoe's perverse island landscape, however, the sea relinquishes its primary role, and the land assumes the trope of otherness. Even the waterspouts are land-based, which may explain their flirtatious peculiarities:

> And I had waterspouts. Oh,
> half a dozen at a time, far out,
> they'd come and go, advancing and retreating,
> their heads in cloud, their feet in moving patches
> of scuffed-up white.

Even these liquid funnels, which should have been beautiful, are disheveled. In spite being lovely "sacerdotal beings of glass" the funnels spout like chimneys. Crusoe's perception refuses the consolations of romantic languages of the sublime and the picturesque. Though risen from the "cloud-dump," his voice drops suddenly into the despair of isolation: "Beautiful, yes, but not much company." This first mention of human companionship forces reconsideration of those recalled human images: the war-torn, anthropomorphized landscape of volcanoes "with their heads blown off," and craters with "their parched throats."

The landscape shrinks to the metaphorical "crater's edge." Not that the lip of the abyss fails in significance, but rather it lacks specificity. From the precariously weighted "company" of the previous stanza (curiously intimate in its naked closure), Bishop withdraws to the public interior, the realm of literary metaphysical speculation and psychological brinkmanship. In spite of the surface, this stanza shields the grieving survivor from prying eyes. Yet the final aside—"So the more / pity I felt, the more I felt at home"—provides the only clue to life before the wreck. Why would pity of all emotional responses evoke memories of "home"? Bishop invents what appears to be one more casual cliché ("to feel at home") in order to fend off while disclosing a wound. "Company" and "home," however, prompt a retreat into the language of displacement and wilderness.

Unlike his eighteenth-century ancestor, Crusoe savors the moment, feeling no need to mark time. At least that is what the returned exile would have us believe from his timeless chronicle. What remains are formal moments sutured by the silence of a life lived and remembered. Each episode confronts a different issue of estrangement and isolation. As if to elude the monotony described—"The sun set in the sea; the same odd sun / rose from the sea"—Crusoe turns to a distillation of his experience with his description of the homely tasks of winemaking and the subsequent drunken flute playing.

The Dionysian ritual mimics the "untidy activity" of "The Bight." Survival requires sustenance and amusement; this moment of giddy inebriation begins the tug of war for recovery. Even intoxication on berry wine ("the awful, fizzy, stinging stuff / that went straight to my head"), however, cannot force the obvious answer to the seemingly rhetorical "Home-made, home-made! But aren't we all?" This rambunctious but momentary stay against despair collapses in another introspective view:

> I felt a deep affection for
> the smallest of my island industries.
> No, not exactly, since the smallest was
> a miserable philosophy.

Unlike the figurative hang "over a crater's edge," this all-too-literal slump prompts a return to an early problem, the reason in fact for this narrative: "None of the books has ever got it right." From the start the poem has promised a corrective by one who knows, the traveler.

But he lacks audience-awareness. His poem begins *in medias res*; not only do the stanza breaks inhibit dramatic completion, but the speaker neglects to match his key answer — "Because I didn't know enough" — with its unsounded "why?" Knowledge failed Crusoe long before his exile. The apparently random disciplines, Greek drama and astronomy, forge associative links with Crusoe's Bacchanalia and his persistent attempts to distinguish himself from the surrounding particulars. The unswerving particularity of the previous inventory scene crumbles into the drifts of snail shells about to become Wordsworthian iris beds. Inaccessibility, unexpectedly coupled with the inappropriateness of his book knowledge, allows Crusoe to associate the "bliss of solitude" to the other island, the one he cannot reach.

If books fail, perhaps salvation will arise from tropes of the elemental or excremental. The sounds and aromas of the gull and goat population impress upon Crusoe his difference from the native inhabitants; enough so that upon recall, at a lifetime's remove, Crusoe still "can't shake / them from [his] ears." He recalls an encounter with this population as a chance to assert his difference, his humanity and imagination:

> When all the gulls flew up at once, they sounded
> like a big tree in a strong wind, its leaves.
> I'd shut my eyes and think about a tree,
> an oak, say, with real shade, somewhere.

Real and somewhere counter the otherness of this experience. How can these creatures be so at home on this burned-over island? Driven by boredom, Crusoe dyes a baby goat to force him into exile:

> One day I dyed a baby goat bright red
> with my red berries, just to see
> something a little different.
> And then his mother wouldn't recognize him.

Displacing his feelings of strangeness upon the natural world by isolating the kid from its mother is Crusoe's ultimate retaliation, but it is a pathetic, cruel, and childish one.

Crippled by the boredom and uncanniness of the island, Crusoe must find another perspective to relieve the two-dimensionality of

this scene; he chooses dreams. Within this sleep-tossed state, appe-
tites surface, demanding to be satisfied. Stranded on the surface,
Crusoe stands unable to relinquish or nourish his interior needs.
How like the child's "immense, sibilant, glistening loneliness" is
Crusoe's

> I'd have
> nightmares of other islands
> stretching away from mine, infinities
> of islands, islands spawning islands,
> like frogs' eggs turning into polliwogs
> of islands, knowing that I had to live
> on each and every one, eventually,
> for ages . . .

The cry sounds the note of the condemned man, sentenced to end-
less, isolated, and isolating pointless endeavor. The nightmarish
term makes the catechistic epigraph to *Geography III* ring prophetic. The lessons of geography prevail, the surface of the planet
asserts its role as dominant trope.

The convulsions of the past nine verse-paragraphs spill over into:

> Just when I thought I couldn't stand it
> another minute longer, Friday came.

Geographically and psychologically confined, Crusoe has withdrawn to the smallest temporal measurement. All knowledge — situ-
ational, personal, investigative, remembered, elemental, physical,
irrational — has proven incomplete, insufficient to alleviate isolation. As if to underscore this painful insight, Crusoe parenthetically stresses that "(Accounts of that have everything all wrong.)"
This dismissal of Defoe's account of master–servant meeting for
religious training not only sounds a corrective to the eighteenth-
century tract, but it also denies this stanza the psychological and
emotional embellishments that would satisfy the conventional social and readerly expectations. After toying with the unnourishing
words *nice* and *friends* Bishop underscores all ambiguities with one
of her famous conditionals: "If only he had been a woman!" Just
as Crusoe and Friday have become a male-bonded couple, Bishop
separates them by pointing to their basic incompatibility in terms
of the requirements of the domestic world:

I wanted to propagate my kind,
and so did he, I think, poor boy.

Friday does, however, supply the missing link between Crusoe and
the uninviting landscape. Indeed, he becomes the bridge to Crusoe's
humanity. In his sheer physicality, Friday stands as the ideal foil to
the introspective gloom. Unlike the alien voice of "Manuelzinho,"
voicing sorrowing amusement but incomprehension, Crusoe knows
the significance of this encounter. Unlike the earlier spectator,
Crusoe means no condescension when he recalls: "—Pretty to
watch; he had a pretty body." The role of admiring and loving
white man resurfaces one more time. Perhaps Melville offers the
shrewdest and funniest episode in such "savage" schooling; Ishmael
tells of his waking sensations:

> Now, take away the awful fear, and my sensations at feeling the
> supernatural hand in mine were very similar, in their strangeness,
> to those which I experienced on waking up and seeing Queequeg's
> pagan arm thrown round me.

Ishmael admires the animal (natural) physicality of this pagan can-
nibal. Like Friday, Queequeg becomes more than a mate; he
reaches into the natural unknown. He bridges that gap in which
"The Moose" remain a visual standoff. Like the earlier "friendships" in American literature—Leatherstocking traveling "far to-
wards the setting sun," Huck planning to "light out for the territory
ahead of the rest"—these interior relationships thrive away from
civilization, off the page.

Unlike its prose ancestors, "Crusoe in England" lacks the pages
of narrative that would supply, conceal, and complete a relationship. It depends rather on the lyric strategies of compression and
surprise. Not only does Bishop cloak the relationship with seemingly cast-off diction—"nice," "friends," "pretty"—but details the
core of the lengthy tale in eleven lines. The stanza must bear the
weight of the attempted and canceled antecedent perspectives,
allowing the echoing "pretty" of the final line to multiply the images recalled. Though avoiding scandalous intimacy, the poem suggests a need for resolution of this new dimension, this superficial
core. Just as a new passage is found, the poem adroitly avoids
closure:

> And then one day they came and took us off.
>
> Now I live here, another island,
> that doesn't seem like one, but who decides?

With a single line, Bishop erases an established life and substitutes the weighted present, allowing both deletion and articulation to stand. An entire history collapses into a sentence, and Crusoe re-establishes the historical, chronological frame, abandoning established formal considerations. The abruptness of the intrusive *And* telescopes narrative elements into staging devices. Only in retrospect does it become clear that *them* and *us*, *then* and *now* form the lyric hinges of the poem, the rhetorical elements that defer narrative in favor of lyric or meditative strategies. The isolation on a physical island has been replaced by the random, careless existential interior remove. Caught between the real and uninteresting of this other island, made so because of the postmortem realities, Crusoe can confer but a visual benediction on those treasured relics of a life. Reticent to handle his memorabilia, he whispers, "My eyes rest on it and pass on."

Though this withdrawal effects perspective, the deferred historicism requires closure. To rebuke the historicism, Bishop details the interment of the dry, lifeless artifacts, shorn of utility significance. All that's left is to tag and display them:

> The local museum's asked me to
> leave everything to them:
> the flute, the knife, the shrivelled shoes . . .
> the parasol that took me such a time
> remembering the way the ribs should go.
> It still will work but, folded up,
> looks like a plucked and skinny fowl.
> How can anyone want such things?

The echoing *still* carries the weight of this reminiscence and linguistically transforms living memories to a *nature morte*, museum artifacts. The narrative of the larger world continues, sometimes violently (as indicated by the volcanic eruption), but Crusoe, looking at his life as if it were a completed work of art, has in effect abandoned the present-tense and consigned the world of experience to memory. If he forswore life "seventeen years ago come March," then how can the poem retrieve the originating spark of this tale? The closure of the poem conceals or reveals its originating image, shelved and in Crusoe's rhetoric, drained of significance; it is the knife that once "reeked of meaning, like a crucifix. It lived." Like the man's old black knife in "At the Fishhouses" (that had "scraped the scales, the principal beauty, / from unnumbered fish . . . / the blade of which is almost worn away" [de-aestheticizing the object]), the tool Crusoe begged and implored "not to break" testifies only to his former existence, as if an artifact that proves that he had lived at one time also proves he no longer does. This last "effect" engenders the entire monologue; the knife testifies both to survival and to loss.

Yet the poem still aches for affirmation of interpretive possibilities that would challenge this failure of correspondences. Scanning the particulars of his life, the weary exile challenges the worth of the evidence: "How can anyone want such things?" As if to ward off possible requests for the offal of experience, the final indelicate historian of Crusoe's psyche intrudes, returning to the emotional crux of the poem:

> —And Friday, my dear Friday, died of measles
> seventeen years ago come March.

Crusoe survives the failure of his emotional life and lingers only to "enumerate old themes." Resigned and reconciled, he faces the necessary disjunctions between knowledge and understanding, knowledge and experience without the saving wisdom of "One Art": "(*Write* it!)"

In the 200 or so lines of this poem, Bishop fully realizes the potential of her language-world, illustrating what her poetry can and cannot know. This vision of wholeness exceeds and violates the visual clarity, the conventions established by her previous poems, which explicitly refuse models of inclusion and unity. The tension of "Crusoe" stems from the interplay between the monumental tropes of landscape and the elusive referential nature of the generative emotional core. The hiatus between stanzas command attention by more than the ordinary segmenting and limiting powers of the stanza break; by spatially marking the silences between place and person, the mind and the heart, they constitute one of the rhetoric strategies of understanding. Apparently transparent clarities of language, and conversational syntax expose a lack of autobiographical plenitude. Unlike the seemingly offhand but calculatingly glib counsel of "One Art," the meditation of "Crusoe" strains against the inarticulation of a powerful self-awareness held under erasure by the rhetorical strategies of the poem.

"The End of March"

"I *always* tell the truth in my poems . . . I always stick as much as possible to what *really* happened when I describe something in a poem." So Bishop told her student Wesley Wehr, and her critics have tended to agree that her poems always attempt to generate moral, intellectual, or emotional veracity. The lyric or dramatic viability of their "truth" depends, however, in large part upon the adequacy of a language that depicts a surface world accessible to the imagination without pretending to affix the boundaries of knowledge. Some critics read Bishop as a poet of technical polish and easily relinquished meaning, so that her justly praised clarity detracts from her ultimate worth, while others see a poet of tortured complexity and ignore the "truth" before them. Yet Bishop's "self-referring fictions" delineate not merely landscapes but viewpoints and values as well. For a concluding look at her trope of the journey, this chapter turns to "The End of March" [G], a poem that provides a late, refined restatement of her aesthetic of reticence. The various itineraries, inventories, and inquiries of her literary past here compress into a weary affirmation of the caught but fluid mundo, and praise for the tone and texture of the phenomenal world.

Like Whitman's "As I Ebb'd with the Ocean of Life," Bishop's poem records "musing" and "gazing" and a "spirit that trails in the lines underfoot, / the rim, the sediment that stands for all the water and all the land of the globe." As in the story "The Sea and Its Shore," life in the flux means occupying the distinct although shifting boundaries between the land and the sea; Bishop shows no desire to cross the Horatian "estranging main." She prefers instead a truncated journey of discovery, the limitations of which are the natural ones of the shore world (visible shore, weather, length, and breadth of the beach) and of her life. Though topically this poem has much in common with Ammons's "Corsons Inlet," the spirit, intensity, and perspective are much closer to Stevens's "Not Ideas About the Thing but the Thing Itself." Bishop, too, sees herself "at the earliest ending of winter," walking a Whitmanesque "rim." "The End of March" demonstrates the remarkable consistency of Bishop's aesthetic of knowledge and surface.

The title defines an interpretive realm of possibility. Bishop locates herself in a specific time of the year, and perhaps time of life. The seasons, shore, planetary influences, the necessary disjunction of people and places, the sensate realities of "our earthly trust," all abide in this poem-as-walk. The central trope of the individual journey marginalizes domesticity and companionship, but both are nonetheless important. The first and last stanzas account for and accommodate fellow travelers and dedicatees Bill Read and John Malcolm Brinnin, who serve as abiding and friendly links to the exterior world. Safely companioned on this chilly beach-trek, Bishop is free to move into the dream-house fantasy without fear of losing touch with actuality.

The staging of "The End of March," like that of "The Monument," requires a continuously shifting stance to track the metaphorically varied geography of the poem. The opening describes a conditional landscape:

> It was cold and windy, scarcely the day
> to take a walk on that long beach.
> Everything was withdrawn as far as possible,
> indrawn: the tide far out, the ocean shrunken,
> seabirds in ones or twos.
> The rackety, icy, offshore wind
> numbed our faces on one side;
> disrupted the formation
> of a lone flight of Canada geese;
> and blew back the low, inaudible rollers
> in upright, steely mist.

>   [CP, 179]

The travelers not only walk against the wind, but seem to violate common sense in doing so. Though the landscape and inhabitants are "withdrawn" and "indrawn," the scene is neither devoid of meaning nor silent. As the ocean — a trope of lyric possibility — shrinks, the shore world — a trope of the historical imagination — expands. When the tide is out, the ocean not at home (cf. "The Moose"), certain kinds of discovery become possible. The elements, which we hear speaking, batter the profiles of the walkers. The "rackety, icy, offshore wind" is audible and tactile as was the "hairy, scratchy, splintery" woods of New Brunswick in "The Moose." The buffeting subjects not only the humans, but also the "lone flight of Canada geese" and "the low, inaudible roller / in upright steely mist." People witness rather than shape this landscape, which is subject to some powerful exterior force.

A meditation upon the described scene follows as Bishop yokes the reality of Duxbury beach to the expected (as least in her world) tropes of form, design, and art. Color, form, impressions of previous discoverers inspire the history of the place:

> The sky was darker than the water
> — *it* was the color of mutton-fat jade.
> Along the wet sand, in rubber boots, we followed
> a track of big dog-prints (so big
> they were more like lion-prints) . . .

The emphatic yet ambiguous pronoun links object to description in a playful manner. Even in its concreteness, "mutton-fat jade," rather than merely particularizing the seaview, widens the poem's range of reference into the realm of the improbable. All objects and travelers on this beach will be consumed by shore-world forces that tend on the one hand to complicate and extend knowledge in rather disconcerting ways, and on the other to eradicate identity. The sand claims impressions — footprints of walkers and prowling beasts — only to eventually relinquish them to the sea, as if all journeys were expendable first-drafts. The parenthetical shift of scale, from dog prints to lion prints, quietly invokes not only a natural hierarchy but an artistic one as well.

Yet while Bishop gestures toward a literary tradition she returns to the language of design and form as she notes the artistic accidentals found about her:

> Then we came on
> lengths and lengths, endless, of wet white string,
> looping up to the tide-line, down to the water,
> over and over. Finally, they did end:
> a thick white snarl, man-size, awash,
> rising on every wave, a sodden ghost,
> falling back, sodden, giving up the ghost . . . .
> A kite string? — But no kite.

Though chaos intrigues Bishop, she always seeks to tame or at
least order it. Unlike the "tide-looped strings of fading shells" in
"Florida," these designs have ordered themselves independently of
the willful waves. The missing kite becomes the true artisan here;
and yet the artifact drifts free of its creator. Bishop demonstrates
her casual mastery of the idiomatic cliché: "a sodden ghost, / falling back, sodden, giving up the ghost," personifying the work of
art that now seems "part of nature" (as Stevens puts it) as well as
"part of us." The unanswerable question of the last line quoted here
("A kite string?") suggests the limitations of such surface worlds by
lack of full evidence for even the simplest occurrences.

The shrunken exteriority of the shore world emphasizes the central tenets of Bishop's own written world. But what if indulging in
the luxury of personal withdrawal she imagines for herself a world
apart from the world? The core of this poem is a dialogue of the
mind with itself as it weighs the appeal of such withdrawal. The
poet applies her familiar surface strategies to the topic of interiority
as retirement from her art:

> I wanted to get away as far as my proto-dream-house,
> my crypto-dream-house, that crooked box
> set up on pilings, shingled green,
> a sort of artichoke of a house, but greener
> (boiled with bicarbonate of soda?),
> protected from spring tides by a palisade
> of — are they railroad ties?
> (Many things about this place are dubious.)

This original and secret dwelling is the interior of the monument,
or of any of Bishop's other works. It is not a fantasy to share with
her walking companions, but rather a self-contained dream. The
exterior of the house as presented here is amusing and suggestive,

but contains an ultimately heartless fantasy of self-exile. This becomes a painfully Thoreauvian kind of imagined luxury, a respite from actuality, a world where "we learn . . . by converse with things." The inverted artichoke house is recognizable but unrealizable, since it represents a possibility Bishop long ago relinquished in making her aesthetic choices. Like the crater-stranded Crusoe, she sounds as if she has had this dreamy discussion with herself many times before. The structure of the poem is the envelope of a recurring but idle dream of a house she can never quite reach — a place, like an epiphany, her poem must turn its back upon.

Moving from the ambiguous exterior to a Spartan interior, Bishop describes an imagined life after (or at least apart from) poetry:

> I'd like to retire there and do *nothing*,
> or nothing much, forever, in two bare rooms:
> look through binoculars, read boring books,
> old, long, long books, and write down useless notes,
> talk to myself, and, foggy days,
> watch the droplets slipping, heavy with light.
> At night, a *grog a l'américaine*.
> I'd blaze it with a kitchen match
> and lovely diaphanous blue flame
> would waver, doubled in the window.

Now the poet's withdrawal matches that of the sea and its shore. Here the rooms (and perhaps even stanzas) would be bare (cf. Crusoe's book full of blanks), the binoculars would narrow and overfocus her vision, her books, notes, and speech would fail — or no longer need — to communicate. She describes an interior world of private ritual and hieroglyphics. The mature Bishop has reached the final waiting room. Unlike the bored Crusoe drinking her "real tea," this exile contemplates with pleasure an idle and pointless retirement.

Now Bishop exits to the exterior reality of this monumental shelter; as always, form comforts her by insisting on necessary connections:

> There must be a stove; there *is* a chimney,
> askew, but braced with wires,
> and electricity, possibly

> — at least, at the back another wire
> limply leashes the whole affair
> to something off behind the dunes.
> A light to read by — perfect! But — impossible.

The poet illuminates the interior by contemplating a reliable exterior. From the chimney's presence she deduces a stove. The limp leash of wire corresponds to the kiteless snarl of kite string. With the addition of a reading light, Bishop comes close to seeing beyond her formal life, the life of letters and work, though in pronouncing the proto-crypto-dream-house "perfect," she marks its impossibility. To accentuate her renunciation of this interior revery, she withdraws to the exterior of the house and to the limits of the walk and of the poem:

> And that day the wind was much too cold
> even to get that far,
> and of course the house was boarded up.

Again, the day is unfit for such an undertaking. "Of course" there would be no access to the interior. As Bishop returns to the exposed exterior of the house, she shields her interior self from its own fantasy.

All journeys define for themselves temporal, geographical, and mortal limits. The companioned return-journey from the interior seeks to position the poet on the shore in the way that the poet has located her sandpiper:

> On the way back our faces froze on the other side.
> The sun came out for just a minute.
> For just a minute, set in their bezels of sand,
> the drab, damp, scattered stones
> were multi-colored,
> and all those high enough threw out long shadows,
> individual shadows, then pulled them in again.

Like the Gentleman of Shalott, the walkers seem only half realized in themselves. The shoreline walk imposes upon them differing land and sea profiles. The echo of "for just a minute" anticipates the shadows to come, which seem momentarily reflected in other objects in the landscape: The stones assume a memorial particularity and then an individuality as the scale shifts, conferring upon them an almost human stature. The shadows become the stones' projections into the world (even as the poet's dream house momentarily projected her interior life into concrete actualization). These shadows are abruptly withdrawn by the sun as Bishop's house was withdrawn by its impossibility.

Finally Bishop finds salvation not in an enduring presence but rather in the observed and lived moment. Unlike the world-weary Lowell of *Day by Day*, Bishop retains (what Lowell considered her key trait) a "tone of large, grave tenderness and sorrowing amusement." Profundity too often suggests unhealthy introspection, so Bishop builds upon exterior incongruities to create a world where description is but one more element, like air or water. In this world description evokes a playful nature sentience:

> They could have been teasing the lion sun,
> except that now he was behind them
> — a sun who'd walked the beach the last low tide,
> making those big, majestic paw-prints,
> who perhaps had batted a kite out of the sky to play with.

The easy tone of the closure reflects the early learning of one whose grandmother "laughed to hide her tears." Speculation and observation, inventories and queries are Bishop's inheritance as well as her strategies, but her retreat from a language of interior fantasy to one of fanciful naturalism indicates how affirmative and central is her poetic of reticence, how crucial it is in shaping the poem as wholes.

Bishop's reflections confirm Wallace Stevens's view of artistic temperament as the poet's congenital world view, as he expresses it in "The Effects of Analogy":

> A man's sense of the world is born with him and persists, and penetrates the ameliorations of education and experience of life. His species is as fixed as his genus. For each man, then, certain subjects are congenital. Now, the poet manifests his personality, first of all, by his choice of subject. Temperament is a more explicit word than personality and would no doubt be the exact word to use, since it emphasizes the manner of thinking and feeling.

The child who saw the relational worth of things, learning early how to experience form, became a poet of exteriority and containment. Striving always for the self-contained work, Bishop demanded of herself the creation of an entity verifiable entirely by the senses. These poetic events require more than appreciation of surface technique; they require acknowledgment of the implications for knowledge inherent in her lyrical strategies, her search for adequate languages of the landscape and the self. The retreat from a longed-for fantasy life in "The End of March" is not a mere psychological aberration, learned early from elders in the habit of concealing their feelings, but a positive aesthetic gesture toward the efficacies of the phenomenological world. Fantasy lives can never be truly shared in the way the concrete and sensuous world can be. Confronting the limitations as well as the excellence of her poems confirms not only her craftsmanship but the beautiful complexities of the apprehensible world for which it is a metaphor.

Notes

Holdings in special collections are noted as follows:

Harvard	Houghton Library, Harvard University
Washington	Olin Library, Washington University
Princeton	Firestone Library, Princeton University
Vassar	Vassar College Library
Rosenbach	Rosenbach Museum and Library, Philadelphia

Preface

p. xi *"identifiable literary entities"* Bishop's passion for literary correspondence is evident in her personal library [Harvard]. A range of models for the literariness of her correspondence is suggested by the following, often heavily annotated (especially the Keats), works: Jane Austen, *Letters, 1796–1817*; *Letters and Memorials of Jane Welsh Carlyle* (3 vols.); Chekhov, *Letters*; Coleridge, *Letters* (2 vols.); *A Selection from Cowper's Letters*; Dickinson, *Letters to Dr. & Mrs. Holland*; Hopkins, *Letters to Robert Bridges*; Henry James, *The Letters* (2 vols.); John Keats, *The Letters* (Rollins ed., 2 vols.); Rilke, *Wartime Letters*; *The Letters of Sydney Smith* (2 vols.); Edmund Wilson, *Letters on Literature and Politics*. As Bishop commented to Wesley Wehr [see "Elizabeth Bishop: Conversations and Class Notes" in *Antioch Review* 39(Summer 1981):320–21]:

> Have you read the Keats letters? I think I enjoy them more than his poetry. He had a wonderful brain and a very strong character. People wrote better letters in those days. Also, you should read Hopkins's letters

to Robert Bridges. They contain some of the best statements I've ever read. His journals—for sheer observations—are superb. He and Marianne Moore are the finest observers I've ever read.

Bishop's letters to May Swenson [Washington], Robert Lowell [Harvard], Marianne Moore [Rosenbach], Jane Dewey [Carbondale], and Kit and Ilsa Barker [Princeton] form significant literary entities in themselves. The exhaustive correspondence with biographer Anne Stevenson [Washington] reveals a poet attentive not only to the presentation of her work but to her place in literary history as well.

Though they serve the obvious function of locating Bishop in tradition and generation, they offer far more as literary property. These letters demand incisive critical treatment as literary works in their own right. The apparent shift in Bishop's poetry from descriptive to narrative seems less unexpected when we realize these strategies complement and coexist throughout her letter-writing career.

p. xi *"A common approach"* The critical preoccupation with "painterly" poems seems to originate with Randall Jarrell. In a review originally published in *Prairie Schooner* (Spring 1963), Jarrell claims:

> Her best poems—poems like "The Man-Moth," "The Fish," "The Weed," "Roosters," "The Prodigal Son," "Faustina, or Rock Roses," "The Armadillo"—remind one of Vuillard or even, sometimes, of Vermeer.

See *The Third Book of Criticism* (New York: Farrar, Straus, & Giroux, 1969), p. 325. Bishop was so appreciative of Jarrell's comparison that she more than once encouraged Anne Stevenson to consider Jarrell's critical gesture as more appropriate than Stevenson's link of Bishop with Andrew Wyeth:

> [re: Stevenson's manuscript] The ONLY thing I didn't like very much, and you guessed I wouldn't before I saw it, was the Wyeth comparison. I know what you mean by it, of course—but I dislike what he stands for in American painting. Randall has said Vuillard—and that is more what I *feel* like, I think . . .
>
> [Washington; November 14, 1964]

Even the most insightful critical gestures grow trite. As of this writing, at least three studies delve into Bishop's poems in search of paint not language. The seductiveness of such an approach is best seen in David Kalstone, *Becoming a Poet: Elizabeth Bishop with Marianne Moore and Robert Lowell* (New York: Farrar, Straus, & Giroux, 1989). In the "Afterword" (the work was unfinished at the time of Kalstone's death), James Merrill notes:

In 1983 David's friend Svetlana Alpers published *The Art of Describing*, a study of seventeenth-century Dutch painting. The book struck him as bearing uncannily upon his own. In particular the polarity between Dutch painters and those of the Italian Renaissance, the latter felt by historians even in our time to be somehow more "important" than the genial natural-ists beyond the Alps—couldn't this be fruitfully applied to a view of Bishop and Lowell? (258)

So apt is this study that it has buttressed another two studies: James McCorkle, *The Still Performance: Writing, Self, and Interconnection in Five Postmodern American Poets* (Charlottesville: University of Virginia Press, 1989), pp. 7–45; Bonnie Costello, *Elizabeth Bishop: Questions of Mastery* (Cambridge: Harvard University Press, 1991). Costello notes the Kalstone biography, but not in connection with Alpers. Her abbreviated "Epilogue" suggests independent discovery of "the revisionary interpretation" of Alpers [256*n*].

p. xi *"constraints of the social"* Such mixed media approaches draw such critics away from the obstinacy of language, thereby deflecting attention from the mediating effect of language itself.

p. xii *"invariably marginalized women"* Rebelling against linkage to Marianne Moore based solely on gender, Bishop counseled her biographer:

> I believe that everyone has the right to interpret exactly as they see fit, of course, so as I said, please do not think I shall be "interfering." My only request of that sort may be quite unnecessary—It is just that I am rather weary of always being compared to, or coupled with, Marianne—and I think she is utterly weary of it, too! We have been good friends for thirty years now—but except for one or two early poems of mine and perhaps some early preferences in subject matter, neither she nor I can see why reviewers always drag her in with me! For one thing—I've always been an umpty-umpty poet with a traditional "ear." Perhaps it is just another proof that reviewers really very rarely pay much attention to what they're reading + just repeat each other.
>
> [Washington; March 18, 1963]

p. xii *"perhaps non-existent faculty"* Feminist critics of Bishop have tended to dismiss the aesthetic implications of Bishop's stand on gender and art. In a letter to Joan Keefe [June 8, 1977; ironically reprinted in *The Norton Anthology of Literature by Women*, ed. Sandra M. Gilbert and Susan Gubar (New York: W. W. Norton, 1985), p. 1739], Bishop reiterates:

Undoubtedly gender does play an important part in the making of any art, but art is art and to separate writings, paintings, musical compositions, etc., into two sexes is to emphasize values in them that are *not* art.

Perhaps if the editors had taken Bishop's commitment to art seriously, they would have caught Bishop's allusion to Matthew 26:58 [KJV] in "Roosters." Instead they gloss "The sun climbs in, / following 'to see the end'" as "probably not a quotation from any particular source, but an expression akin to the expression 'to stay to the bitter end'" (1744). Readers who politicize Bishop at the expense of her art will invariably misread.

p. xiii *"most interesting moment"*   For a range of readings of the Lowell and Bishop affair, see Ian Hamilton, *Robert Lowell: A Biography* (New York: Random House, 1982), pp. 134–37 (Hamilton's reliance upon anonymous informants contributes to the *entre-nous* quality of the biography); see William Doreski, *The Years of Our Friendship: Robert Lowell and Allen Tate* (Jackson: The University Press of Mississippi, 1990), p. 85; Lorrie Goldensohn, *Elizabeth Bishop: The Biography of a Poetry* (New York: Columbia University Press, 1991), pp. 162–91.

Introduction

p. 3 *"Emersonian 'natural facts'"*   Ralph Waldo Emerson, "Nature," in *Emerson: Essays and Lectures*, ed. Joel Porte (New York: The Library of America, 1983), p. 20.

p. 3 *"called 'verifiable' knowledge"*   William James, *Pragmatism* and *The Meaning of Truth* (Cambridge: Harvard University Press, 1978), p. 97.
In *Pragmatism*, James makes the following distinction:

True ideas are those that we can assimilate, validate, corroborate, and verify. False ideas are those we cannot.

p. 4 *"Bishop's 'classical serenity'"*   See Lowell's dust jacket blurb for Bishop's *The Complete Poems* (1969):

I am sure no living poet is as curious and observant as Miss Bishop. What cuts so deeply is that each poem is inspired by her own tone, a tone of large, grave tenderness and sorrowing amusement. She is too sure of herself for empty mastery and breezy plagiarism, too interested for confession and musical monotony, too powerful for mismanaged fire, and too civilized for idiosyncratic incoherence. She has a humorous, commanding genius for picking up the unnoticed, now making something sprightly and right, and now a great monument. Once her poems, each shining, were too few. Now they are many. When we read her, we enter the classical serenity of a new country.

p. 4 *"descendent of Thoreau"*   On the issue of such New England issues of boundaries and identities, see Sharon Cameron, *The Corporeal Self: Allegories of the Body in Melville and Hawthorne* (Baltimore: The Johns Hopkins University Press, 1981), p. 3:

> Yet I wish to suggest that although I concentrate on *Moby-Dick* and Hawthorne's tales, there are connections between the issues I raise here and the heart of our American literary tradition. Thus, alongside *Moby-Dick* and Hawthorne's tales there would be much to say about the way in which other American writers, or works by the same writers, are concerned with identic separations and boundary revisions, are concerned with "third" bodies, are concerned with a barely recognizable corporeality that insistently confuses distinctions between the body of the person and the body of the land.

p. 5 *"Thoreau's 'johnswort'"*   Henry David Thoreau, *Journal*, ed. Bradford Torrey and Francis Allen, 14 vols. (Boston: Houghton Mifflin, 1906), 1:381:

> Well, now, to-night my flute awakes the echoes over this very water, but one generation of pines has fallen, and with their stumps I have cooked my supper, and a lusty growth of oaks and pines is rising all around its brim and preparing its wilder aspect for new infant eyes. Almost the same johnswort springs from the same perennial root in this pasture.

p. 5 *"have repeatedly argued"*   Bishop's aesthetic develops Wallace Stevens's assertion that "Description is an element, like air or water" ("Adagia" in *Opus Posthumous* [New York: Alfred A. Knopf, 1989], p. 200), making it more akin to the "In the Village" world where all the elements "spoke."

p. 5 *"like her fairy"*   For a shrewd assessment of the aesthetic continuities and discontinuities between Marianne Moore and Bishop, see Lynn Keller, *Re-making It New: Contemporary American Poetry and the Modernist Tradition* (Cambridge: Cambridge University Press, 1987), pp. 79–136; for the most eloquent biographical glimpse of the poets, see Kalstone, *Becoming a Poet*, pp. 3–108.

Keller's "The Map" to "Sonnet" overview anticipates and informs Costello's later treatment (For example, see Keller, pp. 108, 136; Costello, p. 242).

p. 6 *"power of icebergs"* Emily Dickinson, *The Letters*, ed. Thomas Johnson, 3 vols. (Cambridge: Harvard University Press, 1958), 3:822.

p. 8 *"is an illumination"* Stevens, "Introduction," *The Necessary Angel* (New York: Alfred A. Knopf, 1951), p. viii.

p. 9 *"Much of Questions"* On the relationship between these memoirs, see my earlier essay, "Robert Lowell and Elizabeth Bishop: A Matter of Life Studies," *Prose Studies* 10 (May 1987), pp. 85–101; Kalstone, *Becoming a Poet*; Goldensohn, *Elizabeth Bishop*.

Chapter 1: Deconstructing Images

p. 16 *"moral and physical"* Jarrell, "Fifty Years of American Poetry" in *The Third Book of Criticism*, p. 325.

p. 17 *"called Bishop's 'thingness'"* John Ashbery, "The Complete Poems: Throughout is this Quality of Thingness," *New York Times Book Review* (1 June 1969):8.

p. 19 *"And moving thro'"* *Poems of Tennyson*, ed. Jerome Hamilton Buckley (Cambridge: Harvard University Press, 1958), p. 26.

p. 19 *"Lewis Carroll-like"* See Allen Tate, "Last Days of Alice" in *Collected Poems, 1919–1976* (New York: Farrar, Straus, & Giroux, 1977), p. 38:

> Whatever light swayed on the perilous gate
> Forever sways, nor will the arching grass,
> Caught when the world clattered, undulate
> In the deep suspension of the looking-glass.

p. 20 *"'[n]othing would give'"* Theodore Roethke, *Collected Poems* (New York: Doubleday, 1966), p. 38.

p. 22 *"unlike Crane's 'rustlings'"* See Crane's "Royal Palm":

Green rustlings more than regal charities
Drift coolly from that tower of whispered light.

*****

Mortality — ascending emerald-bright,
A fountain at salute, a crown in view —
Unshackled, casual of its azured height
As though it soared suchwise through heaven too.

> *The Complete Poems of Hart Crane*
> (New York: Liveright, 1966), p. 167.

pp. 22–23 *"the truth of Emerson's"*   See Emerson, "Circles" in *Essays and Lectures*, p. 403:

There are no fixtures in nature. The universe is fluid and volatile. Permanence is but a word of degrees.

p. 24 *"a Stevensian 'arranging'"*   See Stevens, "The Idea of Order at Key West," *The Collected Poems* (New York: Alfred A. Knopf, 1955), p. 130.

p. 24 *"ghostlier demarcations, keener"*   Stevens, "Idea of Order."

p. 26 *"a Paterian interval"*   See Walter Pater, *The Renaissance*, ed. Donald L. Hill (Berkeley: University of California Press, 1980), p. 190.

p. 27 *"bear the subscript"*   See Jarrell, *Poetry and the Age* (New York: Alfred A. Knopf, 1953), pp. 212–14:

Her work is unusually personal and honest in its wit, perception, and sensitivity — and in its restrictions too; all her poems have written underneath, *I have seen it.* She is so morally attractive, in poems like "The Fish" or "Roosters," because she understands so well that the wickedness and confusion of the age can explain and extenuate other people's wickedness and confusion, but not, for you, your own; that morality, for the individual, is usually a small, personal, statistical, but heartbreaking or heart-warming affair of omissions and commissions the greatest of which will seem infinitesimal, ludicrously beneath notice, to those who govern, rationalize, and deplore . . .

p. 28 *"In 'The Monument'"*   See John Berryman, "The Statue" and "Boston Common" in *Short Poems* (New York: Farrar, Straus, & Giroux, 1965), pp. 4–5, 59–64; Robert Lowell, "For the Union Dead" in *For the Union Dead* (New York: Farrar, Straus, & Giroux, 1964), pp. 70–72.

p. 28 *"is abstract art"*   See Bishop's letter to Anne Stevenson (March 18, 1963; [Washington]):

> You are right about my admiring Klee very much — but as it happens, THE MONUMENT was written more under the influence of a set of *frottages* by Max Ernst I used to own, called *Histoire Naturel.* I am passionately (I think I might say) fond of painting; in fact I'd much rather talk about painting than poetry, as a rule.

Bishop's willingness to "talk about painting [more] than poetry" should have warned critics away from "painterly" approaches to her poems. Her freedom to discuss the visual arts came from their peripheral nature.

p. 32 *"The wilderness rose"*   Stevens, *Collected Poems*, p. 76.

Chapter 2: Romantic Rhetorics

p. 37 *"Or like stout"*   John Keats, *Poetical Works*, ed. H. W. Garrod (Oxford: Oxford University Press, 1956), p. 38.

p. 41 *"Bishop expects her"*   See typescript drafts of "Cape Breton" [Vassar]. Bishop notes in a piece titled "Bird Islands" that:

> Ciboux and Hertford, about six miles off the coast of Nova Scotia. During the war planes practiced dropping bombs on a rock between the two. The sheep pastured on them would get frightened and often stampede in a panic and fall over the cliffs into the sea.

p. 42 *"of the Melvillean"*   See Herman Melville, *Moby-Dick* (New York: W. W. Norton, 1967), Chap. 47: "The Mat-Maker."

p. 42 *"Moore's 'A Grave'"*   Marianne Moore, *Observations* (New York: Dial Press, 1924), p. 60.

p. 42 *" 'Domination of Black' "*   Stevens, *Collected Poems*, p. 8.

p. 44 *"repeatedly shifts its"*   See James McIntosh, *Thoreau as Romantic Naturalist* (Ithaca: Cornell University Press, 1974) for a detailed discussion of Thoreau's "shifting stances" in the natural world with its implications for transcendentalism in general.

p. 45 *"Back to Boston"*   Working title "Back to Boston," 27/403 [Vassar].

p. 51 *"innocence of 'Five"*   See File 27/403 [Vassar].

p. 51 *"As Robert Hass"*   See Hass, "One Body: Some Notes on Form" in *Claims for Poetry*, ed. Donald Hall (Ann Arbor: University of Michigan Press, 1982), p. 152:

> Being and being seen. R. D. Laing says somewhere that small children don't get up at night to see if you're there, they get up to see if *they're* there. . . . Maybe our first experience of our own formation.

p. 52 *"the Poundian periplum"*   See Ezra Pound, *The Cantos* (New York: New Directions, 1972), p. 324.

p. 53 *"domesticity in relation"*   For a useful discussion of domesticity as topic in Bishop, see Helen Vendler, "Domestication, Domesticity and the Otherwordly" in *Modern Critical Views: Elizabeth Bishop*, ed. Harold Bloom (New York: Chelsea House, 1985), pp. 83–96. Once the only essay to make a compelling case for Bishop's place in the canon, it now seems overcommitted to its theme. For example, in introducing "In the Waiting Room":

> No domesticity is entirely safe. As in the midst of life we are in death, so, in Bishop's poetry, in the midst of the familiar, and most especially there, we feel the familiar as the unknowable. This *guerilla attack of the alien*, springing from the very bulwarks of the familiar, is the subject of "In the Waiting Room" (87). [emphasis mine]

A "dentist's waiting room" does not seem to me to be "the very bulwarks of the familiar." In fact, if we are to accept Vendler's extreme depiction, it is just where one would expect the "guerilla attack of the alien."

p. 54 *"claimed of Marianne"*   See "Efforts" [CPr], p. 156.

p. 54 *"I must confess"*   EB to Robert Lowell (December 14, 1957) [Harvard].

p. 54 *"crisis of authorship"*   See my earlier discussion of the rhetorical implications in "Elizabeth Bishop: Author(ity) and the Rhetoric of (Un)-naming," *The Literary Review* 35 (Spring 1992):419–28. My discussion of "otherness and (un)naming" is informed throughout by Kimberly W. Bentson, "I yam what I am: the topos of un(naming) in Afro-American literature" in *Black Literature and Literary Theory*, ed. Henry Louis Gates, Jr. (New York: Methuen, 1984), pp. 151–72.

p. 55 *"the author provides"* Michel Foucault, "What Is an Author?" in Josué Harari, *Textual Strategies: Perspectives in Post-Structuralist Criticism* (Ithaca: Cornell University Press, 1979), p. 151.

p. 56 *"Mrs. Anderson's Swedish"* Stevens, "The Pleasures of Merely Circulating," *Collected Poems*, p. 150. See Vendler's use of the quote in "Domestication," p. 88:

> [U]nderstatement, so common in Bishop, gives words their full weight. As the fact of her own contingency strikes the child, "familiar" and "strange" become concepts which have lost all meaning. "Mrs. Anderson's Swedish baby . . . "

p. 56 *"calls) 'author construction'"* Foucault, p. 151.

p. 59 *"Detect[ing] the sound"* Stevens, "The Woman That Had More Babies Than That," *Opus Posthumous* (New York: Alfred A. Knopf, 1989), pp. 104–5:

> The self is a cloister full of remembered sounds
> And of sounds so far forgotten, like her voice,
> That they return unrecognized. The self
> Detects the sound of a voice that doubles its own,
> In the images of desire, the forms that speak,
> The ideas that come to it with a sense of speech.

p. 59 *"a 'temporal specification'"* See Samuel Beckett, *Proust* (New York: Grove Press, 1957), p. 5.

p. 60 *"(Bishop's working title"* See 27/402 [Vassar].

p. 61 *"I never saw"* D. H. Lawrence, "Self-Pity," *The Complete Poems* (New York: Viking Press, 1971), p. 467.

p. 62 *"These external regions"* Stevens, "Notes Toward A Supreme Fiction," *Collected Poems*, p. 405.

p. 63–64 *"'principle of thrift'"* Foucault, p. 159.

Chapter 3: The Absent Mother

p. 65 *"(or 'pointing,' as"* James, "The Tigers in India" in *The Meaning of Truth*, pp. 198–200.

p. 66 *"When Emerson countered"*   Emerson, *Essays*, p. 491.

p. 66 *"Bishop knows that"*   Thoreau, *Journal*, 1:358.

p. 67 *"I stepped from Plank"*   Emily Dickinson, *The Poems*, ed. Thomas Johnson, 3 vols. (Cambridge: Harvard University Press, 1955), 2:650.

p. 68 *"It is certain"*   Emerson, "Nature" in *Essays*, p. 11.

p. 70 *"As he explains"*   Philippe Ariès, *Centuries of Childhood: A Social History of Family Life*, tr. Robert Baldick (New York: Alfred A. Knopf, 1962), p. 39.

p. 70 *"In Nature he"*   Emerson, "Nature" in *Essays*, p. 10.

p. 70 *"The child asks"*   Emerson, "Experience" in *Essays*, p. 477.

p. 71 *" 'a double awareness' "*   See M. H. Abrams, "Structure and Style in the Greater Romantic Lyric" in *Romanticism and Consciousness*, ed. Harold Bloom (New York: W. W. Norton, 1970), pp. 206–7.

p. 75 *"The scene recalls"*   William Faulkner, *The Sound and the Fury* (New York: Random House, 1956), pp. 46–47.

p. 77 *"Bishop in her"*   EB interview by Elizabeth Spires, *The Paris Review* 80 (Summer 1981):74–75.

p. 78 *"Bishop recalls her"*   See "What the Young Man Said to the Psalmist," *Poetry* 79 (January 1952):212–13.

p. 78 *"Like the Dickinson"*   See Poem 790 in Dickinson, *Poems*, 2:596.

p. 79 *"As Gaston Bachelard"*   See *The Poetics of Space*, tr. Maria Jolas (Boston: Beacon Press, 1969), pp. 4, 5.

p. 81 *"Like the boarding"*   See Robert Frost, "A Servant to Servants" in *The Poetry*, ed. Edward Connery Lathem (New York: Holt, Rinehart, 1969), p. 65.

Chapter 4: The Childish Dusk

p. 85 *"(what William James)"* See James, *The Meaning of Truth*, p. 201.

p. 85 *"what Henry James"* See James, *What Maisie Knew* (New York, 1954), p. 25.

p. 90 *"When Bishop questions"* See EB, "As We Like It," *Quarterly Review of Literature* (Marianne Moore Issue 1948):129-35; rpt. Lloyd Schwartz and Sybil Estess, *Elizabeth Bishop and Her Art* (Ann Arbor: The University of Michigan Press, 1983), p. 279.

p. 95 *"what Clifford Geertz"* See Geertz, "Blurred Genres: The Refiguration of Social Thought" in *Local Knowledge: Further Essays in Interpretive Anthropology* (New York: Harper, 1983), p. 31.

p. 96 *"'I noticed People'"* See Dickinson, *Poems*, 2:805; see Robert Dale Parker, *The Unbeliever: The Poetry of Elizabeth Bishop* (Urbana: University of Illinois Press, 1988), p. 158*n*. Like Parker, I believe that these poems demonstrate "interesting possibilities of influence." Dickinson's poem complements Bishop's apprehension that the poetic calling may be traced to moments when a language must be invented to explain such "disappearances" and "withheld" facts.

p. 98 *"Like the Williams"* See William Carlos Williams, *Paterson* (New York: New Directions, 1963), p. 11.

p. 98 *"Bishop must penetrate"* See Robert Lowell, "91 Revere Street" in *Life Studies* (New York: Farrar, Straus, & Giroux, 1959), pp. 12-13:

> Major Mordecai Myers' portrait has been mislaid past finding, but out of my memories I often come on it in the setting of our Revere Street house, a setting now fixed in the mind, where it survives all the distortions of fantasy, all the blank befogging of forgetfulness. There, the vast number of remembered *things* remains rocklike.

p. 100 *"(reminiscent of Stevens's"* See Stevens, "The Man on the Dump," *Collected*, p. 202.

Chapter 5: Native Knowledge

p. 102 *"an 'experience-distant'"* See Geertz's discussion of Heinz Kohut's anthropological concepts of "experience-near" and "experience-distant" in "'Native's Point of View': Anthropological Understanding," *Local Knowledge*, pp. 57-59.

p. 103 *"Yet Adrienne Rich's"*   For a compelling reconsideration of racial discourse in white American poetry, see Aldon Nielsen, *Reading Race: White American Poets and the Racial Discourse in the Twentieth Century* (Athens: The University of Georgia Press, 1988), esp. Chap. 6, "Recent Poetry and the Racial Other."

p. 103 *"(defined by separate)"*   For complementary discussions of the dialect trap, see Nielsen's "Introduction" for an explanation of "disjunct signifying systems"; see Henry Louis Gates, Jr., "Dis and Dat: Dialect and the Descent" in *Figures in Black: Words, Signs, and the "Racial Self"* (New York: Oxford University Press, 1987), pp. 167–95, for an investigation into "the masking function of dialect."

p. 104 *"'Filling Station' offers"*   Many critics, anxious to decode the sexual subtext, neglect the spirit of the poem. After reading the poem, May Swenson wrote to Bishop:

> [Howard Moss] gave me a copy of this week's issue [of *The New Yorker*] containing your "Filling Station"—which I love. The "dirty dog, quite comfy" and the "big dim doily draping a taboret" are little marvels, for instance, of humor, exact description, and language-play (and several other things I feel but can't catch hold of in words just now). Its wonderful how the poem is funny and serious both, how it points up the foolishness and squalor-trying-to-be-homey features of the people living there, and at the same time is so indulgent of them. The last line is remarkably thought-provoking, making us ask—(B. and I were just discussing it and she thinks the line means the people believe in god just like they believe in doilies, hairy begonias, etc., and I said, no, it means just as the person who waters the plant, etc., loves it, *somebody* loves these people [the poet, as an instance] and, by extension, somebody loves the poet, he being part of "all") which meaning, straight or satirical, shall we take? and the answer, of course, is *both*.
>
> [Washington; December 9, 1955]

See George Starbuck interview with Elizabeth Bishop, *Ploughshares* 3:3–4(1977): 11–29. When GS mentions the "woman's touch" in "Filling Station":

EB: But no woman appears in it at all.
GS: But the pot, the flowers, the . . .
EB: Crocheted doily, yes.
GS: The woman who is "not there," she's certainly an essential subject of the poem.
EB: I never saw the woman, actually. We knew the men there . . .
GS: But the evidence is . . .

EB: I never . . . Isn't it strange? I certainly didn't feel sorry for whoever
crocheted that thing! Isn't that strange?

p. 107 *"what Harold Bloom"*   See Harold Bloom, "Introduction" to
Modern Critical Views: Robert Lowell (New York: Chelsea House,
1987), p. 1:

> From *Life Studies* (1959) on, Lowell took up his own revisionary version
> of William Carlos Williams's rhetorical stance as a defense against his
> own precursors, T. S. Eliot and Allen Tate. This stance, which is in
> Williams a fiction of nakedness, becomes in Lowell a trope of vulnerabil-
> ity. The trope, once influential and fashionable, has become the mark of
> a school of poets who now seem writers of period pieces. . . . By a pro-
> found paradox, it became clear that a guarded, reticent meditation like
> Stevens's "The Poems of Our Climate" could yield endless knowledge of
> both the poet and oneself, whereas Lowell's overtly candid "Waking in
> the Blue" or "Man and Wife" simply impoverished all knowing whatso-
> ever.
> Time therefore seems to have darkened Lowell's aura in the decade
> since his death. Elizabeth Bishop is now firmly established as the enduring
> artist of Lowell's generation, since the canonical sequence of our poetry
> seem to many among us, myself included, to move from Stevens through
> Bishop on to James Merrill and John Ashbery.

p. 110 *"Her correspondence with"*   See EB to MM [February 19, 1940]
cited in Candace W. MacMahon, *Elizabeth Bishop: A Bibliography,
1927–1979* (Charlottesville: University of Virginia Press, 1980), pp.
149–50.

p. 112 *"James) 'true recorder'"*   Ezra Pound, "Henry James" in *Literary
Essays of Ezra Pound* (London: Faber & Faber, 1960), pp. 299–300:

> I take it as the supreme reward for an artist; the supreme return that his
> artistic conscience can make him after years spent in its service, that the
> momentum of his art, the sheer bulk of his processes . . . and leave him
> simply the great true recorder.

p. 112 *"Letters to Robert"*   See Lowell File [Harvard].

p. 113 *"Take from the"*   See Stevens, "The Emperor of Ice-Cream," *Collected*, p. 64.

p. 121 *"Unlike the Wordsworthian"*   See Emerson, *Emerson in His Journals*, ed. Joel Porte (Cambridge: Harvard University Press, 1982), pp.
228–29.

p. 121 *"As she wrote"* MacMahon, *Bibliography*, p. 150.

p. 122 *"The disturbing and"* See Nielsen, *Reading Race*, for the broader implications of "white cultural hegemony" and the "racial other" (4).

Whatever her intentions, Bishop never found a satisfactory way to circumvent the fact of the racial other. Her curiosity was genuine. In a letter to May Swenson [Washington; February 19, 1955]:

> The cook's baby is a clear mauve color — hasn't turned black yet — extremely cute, I think, but one more thing — along with the animals and birds — to worry about — One of Yeats's poems that always seems one of the realest to me is the Song of the Fool:
>
> > "A speckled cat and a tame hare
> > Eat at my hearthstone
> > And sleep there . . .
> >
> > I start out of my sleep to think
> > Some day I may forget
> > Their food and drink." — and I do, all the time.

p. 123 *"not sound as"* See Gates, "Dis and Dat," pp. 182–83:

> There is nothing intrinsically limiting about the use of dialect in poetry, as Sterling Brown proved, as long as dialect is not seen to be mere misspellings of mispronounced words.

p. 123 *"imperfectly heard Holiday"* See Lloyd Schwartz, "Elizabeth Bishop, 1911–1979" in *Elizabeth Bishop and Her Art* (Ann Arbor: University of Michigan Press, 1983), p. 254:

> Her musical taste included Mozart (*not* Beethoven), Cole Porter, and "Fats" Waller. Billie Holiday was a friend ("Songs for a Colored Singer" were written for her). Her favorite example of "perfect" iambic pentameter was: "I hate to see that evenin' sun go down."

Chapter 6: Crusoe at Home

p. 126 *"Bishop's recollections of"* Starbuck interview, p. 18.

p. 127 *"Helen Vendler believed"* See Vendler, "Eight Poets" in *Part of Nature, Part of Us* (Cambridge: Harvard University Press, 1980), p. 349; David Kalstone, "Elizabeth Bishop: Questions of Memory, Questions of Travel" in *Five Temperaments* (New York: Oxford University Press, 1977), pp. 36, 40.

p. 127 *"Adopting the voice"* Though many of Bishop's generation attempted such cross-gender dramatic monologues (Lowell, Jarrell, and Berryman), I have found no correspondence detailing the difficulties of writing in the voice of the "other."

p. 127 *"the glaze of"* See Robert Lowell, "An Interview with Frederick Seidel" [rpt. of *The Paris Review* 25 (Winter–Spring 1961)] in *Collected Prose* (New York: Farrar, Straus, & Giroux, 1987), p. 264:

> [re: "The Mills of the Kavanaughs"] . . . I was writing an obscure, rather Elizabethan, dramatic and melodramatic poem. I don't know how to describe this business of direct experience. With Browning, for instance, for all his gifts — and there is almost nothing Browning couldn't use — you feel there's a glaze between what he writes and what really happened, you feel the people are made up. In Frost you feel that's just what the farmers and so on were like. It has the virtue of a photograph but all the finish of art. That's an extraordinary thing; almost no other poet can do that now.

p. 128 *"In Elizabeth Bishop's"* See Lowell, "An Interview," p. 245.

p. 143 *"Now, take away"* See Melville, "The Counterpane," *Moby-Dick*, p. 32.

p. 145 *"without the saving"* Compare with other aesthetic imperatives: Williams in *Paterson* ("Say it!") and Stevens in "To the Roaring Wind" ("Speak it").

Conclusion: "The End of March"

p. 147 *"I always tell"* See Wehr, "Elizabeth Bishop": 324.

p. 147 *"Yet Bishop's 'self-referring'"* See Isabel G. MacCaffrey, *Spenser's Allegory: The Anatomy of Imagination* (Princeton: Princeton University Press, 1976), p. 10:

> It is often said that self-referring fictions are peculiarly products of the introspective "modern mind." But modernity and self-consciousness are themselves recurrent historical phenomena. Readers of Dante, of Chaucer, of Spenser, know that imagination's most appropriate personification has always been Narcissus.

p. 147 *"Like Whitman's 'As'"* See Walt Whitman, *Leaves of Grass: Comprehensive Reader's Edition* (New York: New York University Press, 1965), p. 254. Like Bloom and Costello, I read the poem through Whitman; unlike Costello, I find nothing of the "grotesque" in evidence here. It seems instead a poem that is exact, measured, and wise where even the fancy seems verifiable.

p. 148 *"Though topically this"* For an extended discussion of the "walk poem," see Roger Gilbert, *Walks in the World: Representation and Experience in Modern American Poetry* (Princeton: Princeton University Press, 1991).

p. 151 *"Thoreauvian kind of"* See Thoreau, *Journal*, 1:142:

> I am pleased to see the landscape through the bottom of a tumbler, it is clothed in such a mild, quiet light, and the barns and fences checker and partition it with new regularity . . . The smith's shop, resting in such a Grecian light, is worthy to stand beside the Parthenon. The potato and grain fields are such gardens as he imagines who has schemes of ornamental husbandry.
>
> If I were to write of the dignity of the farmer's life, I would behold his farms and crops through a tumbler. All the occupations of men are ennobled so.
>
> Our eyes, too, are convex lenses, but we do not learn with the eyes; they introduce us, and we learn after by converse with things.

p. 151 *"I'd like to"* See typescript [Vassar]:

> —That's where I want to retire and
>   do nothing
> in two/bare slanting rooms: just
>   smell the sea,
> look through binoculars, read long,
>   long books, but slowly,
> very slowly,
> talk to myself if I want, and take
>   down useless notes . . .
> Laugh to myself at my own jokes and
>   drink
> a hot rum toddy every night . . .

p. 153 *"Bishop retains (what"* Lowell's blurb for the dustjacket of *The Complete Poems* (1969).

p. 153 *"A man's sense"* See Stevens, *The Necessary Angel*, p. 120.

Works Cited

Abrams, M. H. "Structure and Style in the Greater Romantic Lyric." *Romanticism and Consciousness*. Ed. Harold Bloom. New York: Norton, 1970. Pp. 201–29.

Ammons, A. R. *A Coast of Trees*. New York: Norton, 1981.

———. *Collected Poems 1951–1971*. New York: Norton, 1972.

Ariès, Philippe. *Centuries of Childhood: A Social History of Family Life*. Trans. Robert Baldich. New York: Random House, 1962.

———. *The Hour of Our Death*. Trans. Helen Weaver. New York: Knopf, 1981.

Ashbery, John. "'The Complete Poems': Throughout Is This Quality of Thingness." *New York Times Book Review* 1 June 1969: 8.

Bachelard, Gaston. *The Poetics of Reverie: Childhood, Language, and the Cosmos*. Trans. Daniel Russell. Boston: Beacon, 1969.

———. *The Poetics of Space*. Trans. Maria Jolas. Boston: Little, Brown, 1969.

Beckett, Samuel. *Proust*. New York: Grove Press, 1957.

Bentson, Kimberly W. "I Yam What I Am: The Topos of Un(naming) in Afro-American Literature." *Black Literature and Literary Theory*. Ed. Henry Louis Gates, Jr. New York: Methuen, 1984. Pp. 151–72.

Berryman, John. *Short Poems*. New York: Farrar, Straus, 1964.

Bishop, Elizabeth. "As We Like It." (Spring 1948) *Quarterly Review of Literature* 4 (1948): 129–35.

———. Bishop Archive. Vassar College Library.

———. Bishop–Stevenson File. Washington University Library, Special Collections.

———. *The Collected Prose*. New York: Farrar, Straus, 1984.

173

_____. *The Complete Poems*. New York: Farrar, Straus, 1969.

_____. *The Complete Poems: 1927–1979*. New York: Farrar, Straus, 1983.

_____, trans. *The Diary of "Helena Morley."* New York: Farrar, 1957.

_____. "It All Depends." *Mid-Century American Poets*. Ed. John Ciardi. New York: Twayne, 1950. P. 267.

_____. "The Manipulation of Mirrors." *New Republic* 135 (1956): 23–24.

_____. "What the Young Man Said to the Psalmist." *Poetry* 79 (1952): 212–13.

_____. Bishop, Elizabeth, and May Swenson. Letters. Washington University Library.

Blake, William. *The Poetry and Prose of William Blake*. Ed. David Erdman. New York: Doubleday, 1965.

Bloom, Harold, ed. *Elizabeth Bishop*. New York: Chelsea House, 1985.

_____, ed. *Robert Lowell*. New York: Chelsea House, 1987.

Brown, Ashley. "Elizabeth Bishop in Brazil." *The Southern Review* 13.4 (1977): 688–704.

_____. "An Interview with Elizabeth Bishop." *Shenandoah* 17 (1966): 3–19.

Cameron, Sharon. *The Corporeal Self: Allegories of the Body in Melville and Hawthorne*. Baltimore: Johns Hopkins, 1981.

Costello, Bonnie. *Elizabeth Bishop: Questions of Mastery*. Cambridge: Harvard, 1991.

Crane, Hart. *The Complete Poems of Hart Crane*. New York: Liveright, 1966.

Dickinson, Emily. *Letters*. Ed. Thomas Johnson. 3 vols. Cambridge: Harvard, 1958.

_____. *Poems*. Ed. Thomas Johnson. 3 vols. Cambridge: Harvard, 1955.

Doreski, C(arole) K(iler). "All the Conditions of Existence." *The Literary Review* 27 (1984): 262–71.

_____. "Back to Boston: Elizabeth Bishop's Journeys from the Maritimes." *Colby Library Quarterly* 24 (1988): 151–61.

_____. "Elizabeth Bishop: Author(ity) and the Rhetoric of (Un)naming. *The Literary Review* 35 (Spring 1992): 419–28.

_____. "Robert Lowell and Elizabeth Bishop: A Matter of Life Studies." *Prose Studies* 10 (1987): 85–101.

Doreski, William. *The Years of Our Friendship: Robert Lowell and Allen Tate*. Jackson: Mississippi, 1990.

Emerson, Ralph Waldo. *Emerson in His Journals*. Ed. Joel Porte. Cambridge: Harvard, 1982.

_____. *Essays and Lectures*. Ed. Joel Porte. New York: Library of America, 1983.

Faulkner, William. *The Sound and the Fury.* New York: Random House, 1932.

Foucault, Michel. "What Is an Author?" In *Textual Strategies: Perspectives in Post-Structuralist Criticism.* Ed. Josué Harari. Ithaca: Cornell, 1979.

Frost, Robert. *The Poetry of Robert Frost.* New York: Holt, 1969.

Gates, Henry Louis, Jr. *Figures in Black: Words, Signs, and the "Racial Self."* New York: Oxford, 1987.

Geertz, Clifford. *Local Knowledge: Further Essays in Interpretive Anthropology.* New York: Harper, 1983.

Gilbert, Roger. *Walks in the World: Representation and Experience in Modern American Poetry.* Princeton: Princeton, 1991.

Gilbert, Sandra, and Susan Gubar, eds. *The Norton Anthology of Literature by Women.* New York: Norton, 1985.

Goldensohn, Lorrie. *Elizabeth Bishop: The Biography of a Poetry.* New York: Columbia, 1991.

Hall, Donald, ed. *Claims for Poetry.* Ann Arbor: Michigan, 1982.

Hamilton, Ian. *Robert Lowell: A Biography.* New York: Random House, 1982.

Hass, Robert. "One Body: Some Notes on Form." *Claims for Poetry.* Ed. Donald Hall. Ann Arbor: Michigan, 1982.

James, Henry. *What Maisie Knew.* New York: Doubleday, 1956.

James, William. *Pragmatism* and *The Meaning of Truth.* Cambridge: Harvard, 1975.

Jarrell, Randall. *Poetry and the Age.* New York: Knopf, 1953.

———. *The Third Book of Criticism.* New York: Farrar, 1969.

Kalstone, David. *Becoming a Poet: Elizabeth Bishop with Marianne Moore and Robert Lowell.* New York: Farrar, 1989.

———. *Five Temperaments.* New York: Oxford, 1977.

Keats, John. *Poetical Works.* Ed. H. W. Garrod. Oxford: Oxford, 1956.

Keller, Lynn. *Re-making it New: Contemporary American Poetry and the Modernist Tradition.* Cambridge: Cambridge, 1987.

Lawrence, D. H. *The Complete Poems.* New York: Viking, 1971.

Lowell, Robert. *Collected Prose.* New York: Farrar, Straus, 1987.

———. *For the Union Dead.* New York: Farrar, Straus, 1964.

MacCaffrey, Isabel. *Spenser's Allegory: The Anatomy of Imagination.* Princeton: Princeton, 1976.

MacMahon, Candance W. *Elizabeth Bishop: A Bibliography, 1927–1979.* Charlottesville: Virginia, 1980.

McCorkle, James. *The Still Performance: Writing, Self, and Interconnection in Five Postmodern American Poets.* Charlottesville: Virginia, 1989.

McIntosh, James. *Thoreau as Romantic Naturalist.* Ithaca: Cornell, 1974.

Melville, Herman. *Moby-Dick.* New York: Norton, 1967.

Moore, Marianne. *Observations.* New York: Dial, 1925.

Nielsen, Aldon. *Reading Race: White American Poets and the Racial Discourse in the Twentieth Century.* Athens: Georgia, 1988.

Ostroff, Anthony, ed. *The Contemporary Poet as Artist and Critic.* Boston: Little, Brown, 1964.

Parker, Robert Dale. *The Unbeliever: The Poetry of Elizabeth Bishop.* Urbana: Illinois, 1988.

Pater, Walter. *The Renaissance: Studies in Art and Poetry.* Ed. Donald Hill. Berkeley: California, 1980.

Pound, Ezra. *The Cantos.* New York: New Directions, 1972.

_____. *The Literary Essays of Ezra Pound.* Ed. T. S. Eliot. London: Faber & Faber, 1954.

Roethke, Theodore. *Collected Poems.* New York: Doubleday, 1966.

Schwartz, Lloyd, and Sybil P. Estess, eds. *Elizabeth Bishop and Her Art.* Ann Arbor: Michigan, 1983.

Seidel, Frederick. "Interview with Robert Lowell." *Paris Review* 25 (1961): 56–95; rpt. Lowell, *Collected Prose.*

Spires, Elizabeth. "Interview with Elizabeth Bishop." *Paris Review* 80 (1981): 56–83.

Starbuck, George. "Interview with Elizabeth Bishop." *Ploughshares* 3.3–4 (1977): 11–29.

Stevens, Wallace. *Collected Poems.* New York: Knopf, 1954.

_____. *The Necessary Angel.* New York: Knopf, 1951.

_____. *Opus Posthumous.* Ed. Milton J. Bates. New York: Knopf, 1989.

Stevenson, Anne. *Elizabeth Bishop.* New York: Twayne, 1966.

Tate, Allen. *Collected Poems, 1919–1976.* New York: Farrar, 1977.

Tennyson, Lord Alfred. *Poems of Tennyson.* Ed. Jerome Hamilton Buckley. Cambridge: Harvard, 1958.

Thoreau, Henry David. *Journals.* Ed. Bradford Torrey and Francis Allen. 14 vols. Boston: Houghton Mifflin, 1906.

Travisano, Thomas J. *Elizabeth Bishop: Her Artistic Development.* Charlottesville: Virginia, 1988.

Wehr, Wesley. "Elizabeth Bishop: Conversations and Class Notes." *Antioch Review* 39 (1981): 319–28.

Whitman, Walt. *Leaves of Grass: Comprehensive Reader's Edition.* New York: New York, 1965.

Williams, William Carlos. *Paterson.* New York: New Directions, 1963.

Index

177

Gramley Library
Salem College
Winston-Salem, NC 27108